The Official NHL
Toronto Maple Leafs
Quiz Book

The Official NHL Toronto Maple Leafs Quiz Book

Edited by
Dan Diamond

Questions by
James Duplacey

Research by
Ralph Dinger

M&S

Toronto   New York   London

CANADIAN CATALOGUING IN PUBLICATION DATA

Diamond, Dan
  The official NHL Toronto Maple Leafs quiz book

ISBN 0-7710-0166-5

1. Toronto Maple Leafs (Hockey team) – Miscellanea. I. Title.

GV848.T6D5 1993   796.962′64′09713541   C93-094852-1

Cover design by Sari Ginsberg
Typesetting by M&S

Cover photo credits (clockwise from top): Turk Broda (Hockey Hall of Fame),
Bobby Baun (Hockey Hall of Fame – Frank Prazak Collection), Leafs-Bruins
game/1933 (Hockey Hall of Fame), Syl Apps (Hockey Hall of Fame –
Imperial Oil Turofsky Collection), Doug Gilmour (Hockey Hall of Fame –
Doug MacLellan)

Text photos: NHL Publishing

Printed and bound in Canada

McClelland & Stewart Inc.
The Canadian Publishers
481 University Avenue
Toronto, Ontario
M5G 2E9

1 2 3 4 5   97 96 95 94 93

Contents

Note: Special quizzes and puzzles are scattered throughout the book.

1

Between the Pipes

A LARGE PART OF THE SUCCESS OF THE TORONTO Maple Leafs throughout the years has been the team's ability to acquire exceptional goaltending. Many of the NHL's all-time great "money" goaltenders – Broda, Bower, Sawchuk, Fuhr – have played in Toronto, on-ice artists who turned up their performance a notch when the game was on the line. A large measure of the credit for the franchise's success can be attributed to the coaching staffs of the great Leaf teams, who implemented a system that focused on team defence and propitious offense. The success of the 1992-93 Maple Leaf club was a direct result of new coach Pat Burns developing an approach that limited the opposition to one scoring chance before the puck was cleared from the defensive zone.

Of course, the system only works when you have top-notch netminders, and Toronto has always been able to find that quality goalie. The first Leaf trade in franchise history involved a goaltender, and the scouting staff from the team's inception to the present day have always had a keen eye for spotting talent between the pipes. Indeed, whenever the franchise has faltered – in the mid-1950s, early 1970s and 1980s – part of the problem has been the lack of a dominant netminder.

The Maple Leafs, who rose from the ashes of the St. Patricks franchise in 1927, were born with the capable John Ross Roach as the team's number-one netminder, but he was quickly replaced by Lorne Chabot. Chabot had been scouted and signed by Conn Smythe from the Allan Cup-winning Port Arthur Bearcats when Smythe was still managing the expansion New York Rangers. Since that time, the Leafs have employed a number of Hall-of-Fame goaltenders, including Turk Broda, Harry Lumley, Johnny Bower, Terry Sawchuk, Jacques Plante, and Bernie Parent. In fact, eight of the NHL's top fifteen career shutout leaders have worn a Maple Leafs' jersey sometime during their career.

Although the Leafs have usually employed a Hall-of-Fame goaltender to capture the Stanley Cup, there have been a couple of notable exceptions. In 1932, the Maple Leafs captured their first Cup with Lorne Chabot in nets. Despite recording 73 career shutouts and winning the Stanley Cup with a pair of teams, Chabot has yet to find his way into the Hockey Hall of Fame, an odd oversight on the part of the nominating committee since he is the only goalie in the top ten shutout leaders excluded. In 1945, Frank "Ulcers" McCool wrote his name into the NHL record books with a memorable performance against the Detroit Red Wings, the only post-season action in his brief career.

The primary focus for the new regime at Maple Leaf Gardens has been to restore pride in the franchise from the goal-line out. Under the astute eye of hockey mastermind Cliff Fletcher, the club has quickly regained its place among the league's elite franchises. It's no surprise that Fletcher's first order of business was to secure a top-line goaltender to solidify the last line of defence. The acquisition of Grant Fuhr gave the Leafs their first quality goaltender since the departure of Mike Palmateer. Fuhr did an admirable job until rookie Felix Potvin was experienced enough to tackle the number-one job. Now, with Potvin on board, the Leafs' goaltending picture seems clear for years to come.

Questions

1. In 1992-93, Felix Potvin became only the fourth Leafs goaltender to be nominated for the Calder Trophy as the league's best freshman. One Leafs goalie has won the award and two others have finished in the runners-up spot. Name them.

2. Name the goalie who, in only his third game as a Leaf, shut out the Chicago Black Hawks on national TV and thwarted Bobby Hull's attempt to score his record-breaking 51st goal.

3. Who holds the Leafs' record for assists by a goaltender in a single season?

4. Name the three former Maple Leaf goaltenders who became general managers in the NHL.

5. Name the former Leafs goalie who won the AHL's playoff MVP award in 1991-92.

6. During the 1932-33 season, the Leafs were forced to use three defencemen in goal. Can you name this trio of black and blue blueliners?

7. Name the former Leaf goaltender who set an NHL record with three assists in a single game.

8. Name the last Leafs goaltender to play in every game during the regular season. For added bonus, give the year.

9. Only two goalkeepers in Leaf history have been traded then reacquired later. Name the travelling duo.

10. The second goaltender to regularly wear a facemask in the NHL later spent three seasons with the Leafs. Can you name this masked marvel?

11. In 1967-68, the six new expansion teams employed a total of 15 goaltenders. Five of those goalies played, or would play, for the Leafs. Name this quintet.

12. Name the first European-trained goaltender to play goal for the Maple Leafs.

13. In the first trade in Maple Leafs history, Conn Smythe exchanged goaltenders with another NHL club. Name the goaltenders and the other team involved.

14. Name the first Maple Leafs goaltender to allow a penalty-shot goal.

15. In the mid-1930s, Conn Smythe went to a Windsor-Detroit junior game looking to sign a young goaltender named Earl Robertson. Instead, he signed another goaltending prospect. Who was this untapped gem?

16. Since the universal amateur/entry draft was introduced in 1969, the Leafs have never selected a goalie in the first round. In fact, they have drafted only one

goalie in the second round. Name the goalie and the year he was drafted.

17. From 1937 to 1949 (with the exception of the years he was in the army) Turk Broda missed only one game. Name the goalie who replaced him in that lone contest.

18. The Toronto Maple Leafs were the first team to introduce the two-goaltender system. What was the year and who were the pair of puck-stoppers?

19. Name the Maple Leafs goaltender who once faced 65 shots in a single game. What year did the barrage take place and how many goals did he allow?

20. Since the NHL expanded in 1979-80, only two Maple Leafs goaltenders have won 25 games in a season. Name the goalies and the year they turned the trick.

21. The last goaltender to win the Hart Trophy as the NHL's MVP once played for the Leafs. Who was this most valuable addition?

22. Name the Leaf farmhand who was forced to play goal for the St. Catharines Saints in a game against the Adirondack Red Wings.

23. In one of his stranger antics, Leaf owner Harold Ballard once ordered that a certain goaltender's beard be airbrushed from a team picture. Name the whiskered goalie.

24. Name the goaltending tandem that finished second to Worsley and Vachon in the Vezina Trophy race in 1968.

25. Who holds the Leafs record for shutouts in a single season and how many zeros did he record?

26. Name all five Toronto Maple Leafs goaltenders to win the Vezina Trophy while with the Leafs.

27. Who was in nets for the Leafs when they captured the Stanley Cup in 1962?

28. Since the Leafs last won the Vezina Trophy in 1965, five Vezina Trophy winners have played for the Leafs. Who are the honoured goalies?

29. During the 1983-84 campaign, the Leafs called up two goaltenders from the junior ranks. Who were the under-age youngsters and what junior teams did they come from?

30. Name the Detroit Red Wings trainer who once played in goal for the Leafs.

31. Through the years, two Edwards's, two Parents, two Smiths and two Wilsons have tended goal for Toronto. Can you supply these surnames with their first names?

32. Name the former Leaf goalie who coached back-to-back Memorial Cup winners.

33. Who backstopped the Leafs to their first Stanley Cup title?

34. This goaltender, who started his career with the Leafs, led all playoff goaltenders in victories twice during the 1970s. Can you name him?

Answers

1. Frank McCool won the Calder in 1944-45, while Al Rollins (1950-51) and Ed Chadwick (1956-57) finished as runners-up.

2. Bruce Gamble blanked the Hawks 5-0 to record his second consecutive shutout in only his third game in the Leafs' net.

3. Mike Palmateer recorded five assists in 1978-79.

4. Baz Bastien (Pittsburgh), Ed Johnston (Hartford), and Gerry McNamara (Toronto).

5. Allan Bester led the Adirondack Red Wings to the AHL championship and captured the Butterfield Trophy as playoff MVP.

6. Alex Levinsky, Red Horner, and King Clancy all tended goal during the 1932-33 campaign.

7. Jeff Reese recorded three assists for Calgary during the 1992-93 season.

8. Ed Chadwick played the entire 70-game schedule in 1957-58.

9. Ben Grant was traded to the New York Americans in 1930 and later returned to Toronto in 1943. Mike Palmateer, traded to Washington in 1980, finished his career in Toronto.

10. Don Simmons, the second goaltender to regularly wear a facemask, recorded shutouts in his first two games wearing a mask on January 10, 1960 (4-0 over Toronto) and January 14, 1960 (6-0 over the New York Rangers). He later played for Toronto from 1961 to 1965.

11. Terry Sawchuk (Los Angeles), Gary Smith (Oakland), Bernie Parent (Philadelphia), Doug Favell (Philadelphia), and Cesare Maniago (Minnesota) all wore the Leafs' blue and white.

12. Jiri Crha played a total of 69 games with the Leafs from 1979 to 1981.

13. The Leafs sent John Ross Roach to the New York Rangers for Lorne Chabot.

14. George Hainsworth, who also stopped the first penalty shot against a Maple Leafs goaltender, allowed

a goal by Bert Connelly of the New York Rangers on January 16, 1936.

15. Smythe saw Turk Broda playing for the Detroit juniors and signed him for the Leafs.

16. Felix Potvin was selected in the second round (31st overall) of the 1990 Entry Draft.

17. In 1939-40, with Broda struggling, Conn Smythe brought up youngster Phil Stein, who was magnificent in a 2-2 overtime tie with the Bruins. Stein was scheduled to start the next game as well, but was hit in the face by a shot during the warm-ups. Broda had to replace him, and Stein never played another game in the NHL.

18. Al Rollins and Turk Broda shared netminding duties during the 1950-51 season.

19. Allan Bester, in his first season in the NHL, stopped 60 of 65 shots (including 32 saves in the second period) against the Hartford Whalers on March 15, 1984.

20. Grant Fuhr won 25 games in 1991-92, Felix Potvin won 25 games during the 1992-93 season.

21. Jacques Plante, who won the Hart Trophy with Montreal in 1962, played for the Leafs for 2½ seasons from 1970 to 1972.

22. Centreman Norm Aubin, who played 69 games for the Leafs in his career, was forced to go into the net for Toronto's farm team in St. Catharines after starter Vince Tremblay was injured. He allowed five goals in a 6-3 loss.

23. Gord McRae, who was sporting a beard during the 1977-78 season, appeared clean shaven for the team's Christmas card after Ballard ordered his 1978 face replaced with a picture of his 1977 face.

24. Johnny Bower and Bruce Gamble finished second in goals-against but the Leafs still missed the playoffs.

25. Harry Lumley recorded 13 shutouts in 1953-54.

26. Turk Broda (1941, 1948), Al Rollins (1951), Harry Lumley (1954), Johnny Bower (1961), and Terry Sawchuk with Johnny Bower (1965).

27. Don Simmons replaced an injured Johnny Bower in the fourth game of the 1962 finals, and played in the fifth and sixth games as the Leafs won their first Cup in 11 years.

28. Jacques Plante (1969), Bernie Parent (1974-1975) Don Edwards (1980), Michel Larocque (1976-1979, 1981), and Grant Fuhr (1988) all won the Vezina Trophy.

29. Ken Wregget from Lethbridge of the WHL and Allan Bester from Brantford of the OHL both played for the Leafs at the age of 19.

30. On January 22, 1956, Wings trainer Ross "Lefty" Wilson replaced Leafs goalie Harry Lumley in the Toronto nets. Wilson, who also substituted for Boston and Detroit during his "career," didn't allow a goal in his 13 minutes in the Leafs' nets.

31. Don and Marv Edwards, Bernie and Bob Parent, Al and Gary Smith, and Lefty and Dunc Wilson.

32. Turk Broda coached the Toronto Marlboros to the Memorial Cup in 1954-55 and 1955-56.

33. Lorne Chabot, whom Conn Smythe originally signed for the New York Rangers in 1927, won the second Stanley Cup of his career in 1931-32.

34. Gerry Cheevers, who led all goalies in post-season wins in 1970 and 1972, played two games for the Leafs in 1961-62.

Name the Nicknames

All these nicknamed heroes played between the pipes for the Leafs. Match the nicknames with the real names on the right. Answers on page 124.

1.	"China Wall"	a.	Walter Broda
2.	"Suitcase"	b.	Gerry Cheevers
3.	"Ernie"	c.	Mark Laforest
4.	"Uke"	d.	Michel Larocque
5.	"Turk"	e.	Harry Lumley
6.	"Cat"	f.	Allan Bester
7.	"Bunny"	g.	Gary Smith
8.	"Apple Cheeks"	h.	Johnny Bower
9.	"Ulcers"	i.	Ken McCauley
10.	"Tubby"	j.	Jacques Plante
11.	"The Popcorn Kid"	k.	Frank McCool
12.	"Jake the Snake"	l.	Felix Potvin
13.	"Chabotsky"	m.	Mike Palmateer
14.	"Trees"	n.	Lorne Chabot
15.	"Cheesy"	o.	Terry Sawchuk

2

On the Blueline

THEIR NAMES CONSTITUTE A VIRTUAL HALL OF FAME roster: Horton, Kelly, Stanley, Pronovost, Pratt, Clancy, Horner, and Day. These are the men who led the Maple Leafs to eleven Stanley Cup championships and six Vezina Trophies. They are the defencemen who molded the Maple Leaf team into one of hockey's most storied franchises.

Although the Leafs have been blessed over the years with exceptional talent, they have always depended on a total team effort for their success. Never a dominant offensive team, the Leafs have constantly relied on opportunistic scoring, sometimes at the expense of their defensive duties. When that was the case, the blueliners would bail them out. The Leafs were renowned for having the toughest, and meanest, rearguards in the NHL. From the rambunctious Red Horner and Bingo Kampman in the club's early years to the workhorse efforts of

Jamie Macoun and Sylvain Lefebvre on the current team, the backbone of the Maple Leafs' success has always been their dominant defence.

When Conn Smythe and his group of investors purchased the team in February 1927, Smythe's first instructions to interim coach Alex Romeril was to shift Hap Day from forward to defence. Although Day went on to become one of the league's finest rearguards, Smythe knew the Leafs needed another top-notch defenceman, so he purchased King Clancy from the Ottawa Senators. Toronto's fearsome trio of Horner, Day, and Clancy launched the Leafs to their first four trips to the Stanley Cup finals.

In the 1940s, the Leafs won five Stanley Cup titles and once again the defence was an overpowering factor in the team's success. Only one of the Leafs regular blueliners during the decade – Babe Pratt – would go on to the Hall of Fame, but foot soldiers like Garth Boesch, Bill Barilko, Bill Juzda, and Gus Mortson were no-nonsense defenders who beat 'em in the alley and on the ice.

During the 1950s, Toronto hockey fans experienced the first dry period in Maple Leaf history. Marc Reaume, Jim Morrison, and captain Jim Thomson were all capable NHL veterans, but a system to take advantage of their talents was never in place. By the time Punch Imlach arrived in 1958, Carl Brewer, Bob Baun, and Tim Horton had been brought up through the farm system, and Allan Stanley had been obtained from the Boston Bruins. This quartet of talent would lead the Leafs into their last great era, four Stanley Cups and six final-round appearances in nine seasons during the 1960s.

Since the expansion of 1967, the role of the blueliner in

the NHL has changed dramatically. Defencemen are now expected to contribute offensively as well as defensively by quarterbacking the powerplay, then recovering to secure their own end. The days when an NHL team could depend on four "stay-at-home" defenders has passed, leaving those teams who were slow to adjust behind.

Despite not having won the Stanley Cup in 26 seasons, the Leafs have nurtured some outstanding blueliners. Borje Salming was a six-time NHL All-Star and holds most of the team's offensive marks for defencemen. Ian Turnbull was a notable offensive contributor from the blueline who set an NHL record for rearguards with five goals in a single game. The current crop of defenders, led by Dave Ellett, Todd Gill, and Jamie Macoun, is as sound as any in the game, while talented youngsters like Drake Berehowsky, Matt Martin, and Janne Gronvall await their chance to contribute to one of the league's most promising up-and-coming teams.

Questions

1. The first man to captain the Toronto Maple Leafs was a defenceman. Name him.
2. This defenceman led the NHL in penalty minutes in each of his last eight NHL seasons. Can you identify this sin-bin king?
3. Often called the strongest man in the NHL, he was equally famous for his "bearhugs" as he was for his blueline efficiency. Name him.
4. Two defencemen have scored Stanley Cup-winning

goals for the Leafs. Can you name these playoff heroes and the years in which they gained their fame?

5. Although no Leaf blueliner has won the Norris Trophy, four Toronto defencemen have come in second. Can you name this quartet of bridesmaids?

6. An outstanding lacrosse player who was originally scouted by Conn Smythe, this defenceman arrived in Toronto from the Detroit Red Wings in 1938. Name this two-sport star.

7. The winners of the top defenceman award in the Western Hockey League from 1981 to 1985 have all played for the Leafs. Can you name this quintet of blueline award winners?

8. In game six of the 1967 Stanley Cup finals, with the Leafs leading Montreal 2-1 in the final minute, the Habs forced a face-off in the Leafs' zone and pulled goaltender Gump Worsley for an extra attacker. Toronto coach Punch Imlach sent a defenceman over the boards to take this crucial draw, even though he hadn't taken a face-off in three seasons. Name the crafty defender who won the draw and sealed the Leafs' Cup victory.

9. This pair of Leafs defencemen jumped to the same WHA team in 1972 and became two of only seven players to play for the same team for the entire seven-year duration of the rival league. Name the Maple Leaf defectors.

10. Name the Leaf defenceman traded to the Detroit Red Wings for Red Kelly.

11. Although no Maple Leaf has won the Norris Trophy,

one recipient began his career in Toronto. Name him, the year he captured the award, and the team he was with.

12. Name the last Leafs defenceman to play at least 70 games in a season and NOT score a goal.

13. The early 1970s were a period of transition for the Maple Leafs, especially along the blueline. In 1972-73, Toronto employed three defencemen who never played for the team again. Can you name these three "unknowns"?

14. In the early 1960s, the Leafs played the "clutch and grab" game to perfection. One Toronto rearguard played it better than others because he removed the palms from his gloves, prompting a rule change by NHL President Clarence Campbell to outlaw the practice. Name the guilty individual.

15. The last defenceman to win back-to-back Stanley Cups with different teams played with the Leafs on the back end of that accomplishment. Name the blue-liner.

16. This Leafs defenceman jumped to the NHL after only ten games of junior. Name the quick climbing rear-guard.

17. Name two current Leafs defencemen to jump directly to the NHL from college without playing in the minors.

18. During the 1970s, only one American-born defence-man suited up for the Leafs. He was the son of one of the NHL's all-time great rearguards. Can you identify him?

19. Two Leaf blueliners share the team record for most

appearances on the regular-season All-Star Team. Name the pair and the number of times each were selected to the league's All-Star squad.

20. Who was the first Leaf defenceman to earn a berth on the All-Star Team?

21. In the first Amateur Draft in 1963 (before the Universal Amateur Draft in 1969), the Leafs selected a young rearguard from Toronto's Neil McNeil High School who later played 13 seasons with the team. Name the student blueliner.

22. This defenceman, who started his career with the Leafs, became the first rearguard in NHL history to score 20 goals in a season. Can you name this sharpshooting blueliner?

23. Name the first American-born defenceman to play for the Leafs. Who was the first European-born rearguard? Who was the first Iron-Curtain defender?

24. Name the Leafs defenceman whose involvement with the first NHL Players Association led to his release.

25. This former Leafs defenceman went onto become a general manager in the NHL. Can you name him?

26. This Hall of Fame defenceman had already played 15 seasons in the NHL when he joined the Leafs. He led them to one Stanley Cup in his five seasons along the blueline. Name him, if you can.

27. A 37-year-old three-time winner of the Norris Trophy arrived in Toronto in one of the oddest trades ever arranged by Punch Imlach. Name the esteemed defenceman.

28. This rough 'n' tough Leafs defenceman was the first

Leaf player to lead the NHL in penalty minutes in his rookie season. Name the bad basher.

29. This Leaf defenceman set an odd team mark by wearing five different numbers in his six full seasons with the team in the mid-1950s. Can you tell the name of this player without a program?

30. This former Leafs defenceman was elected to the Hockey Hall of Fame as a builder for his outstanding contribution to the AHL and has been honoured as a recipient of the Lester Patrick Trophy. Who was he?

31. This defenceman scored one of the most famous goals in Leafs history while playing with a broken ankle. Name the brave warrior.

32. In the 1981-82 season, the Leafs started the campaign with three "kid" defencemen. Can you name the baby-faced trio and give their ages?

33. This defenceman, who started his career with the Leafs, returned to the organization as a minor league player-coach in 1991-92 and earned an AHL Second Team All-Star berth. Who was this talented blueliner?

34. This defenceman was the first Soviet-trained player to suit up for the Leafs. Can you name him?

35. This promising youngster was the Canadian Hockey League's defenceman of the year in 1992. Name him.

36. Another young prospect for the Leafs helped the University of Maine win the school's first NCAA hockey championship. Can you identify this educated blueliner?

37. This popular rearguard was the last Maple Leaf to play without a helmet. Name him.

38. Although this Finnish-born defenceman has yet to play for the Leafs, he was named as the outstanding defenceman at the 1992 World Junior Hockey Championships. Can you name him?
39. Name the three Leafs defencemen to record at least 10 assists in a single playoff season.
40. This defenceman is the only Maple Leaf rearguard to win the Hart Trophy as the NHL's MVP. Can you remember his name?

Answers

1. Clarence "Happy" Day, pharmacist turned hockey hero, was the first captain of the Maple Leafs.
2. Red Horner, who succeeded Hap Day as captain of the Leafs, was the NHL's "bad boy" from 1932-33 to 1939-40.
3. Tim Horton, who debuted with the Leafs during the 1949-50 season, broke up many on-ice confrontations with his "Horton Hug."
4. Walter "Babe" Pratt in 1945 (game seven, 12:14 of the third period) and Bill Barilko in 1951 (game five, 2:53 of overtime) both scored the Cup-winners for the Leafs
5. Allan Stanley (1960), Carl Brewer (1963), Tim Horton (1964, 1969), and Borje Salming (1977, 1980) all earned second-place ratings in the Norris Trophy race.
6. Bucko McDonald was discovered by Conn Smythe, who happened to mention his name to Detroit GM

Jack Adams, who immediately signed McDonald. Smythe exacted his revenge by stealing Turk Broda from under Adams' nose in 1935.

7. Jim Benning (1981), Gary Nylund (1982), Gary Leeman (1983), Wendel Clark (1984), and Bob Rouse (1985) were all selected as the WHL's outstanding defenceman and they have all worn the maple leaf in Toronto.

8. Allan Stanley, one of Imlach's "old pappy" guys, won the faceoff from Jean Beliveau, allowing George Armstrong to score the insurance goal in the Leafs' 3-1 Cup-clinching victory.

9. Rick Ley and Brad Selwood played for the New England Whalers for the entire seven-year lifespan of the WHA. Ley later played for Hartford in the NHL while Selwood finished his career with the Los Angeles Kings. The other lifetime WHAers who played with just one club were Bobby Hull (Winnipeg), Al Hamilton (Edmonton), J.C. Tremblay (Quebec), Joe Daley (Winnipeg), and Richard Brodeur (Quebec).

10. Marc Reaume, who played only 47 games for the Red Wings, was sent to Motown for Red Kelly, who helped the Leafs win four Cups in the 1960s.

11. Randy Carlyle, who spent two seasons with the Leafs, won the Norris Trophy with the Pittsburgh Penguins in 1981.

12. Bob "Big Daddy" McGill was held goal-less in 72 games during the 1984-85 season.

13. Larry McIntyre, John Grisdale, and Joe Lundrigan were the "forgettable" trio.

14. Carl Brewer was the "grabber" in question.

15. Al Arbour, who also won Cups with Detroit as a player and the New York Islanders as a coach, won the championship with Chicago in 1961 and Toronto in 1962.

16. Al Iafrate, the Leafs' first choice in the 1984 Entry Draft, played 10 games with the Belleville Bulls after the 1984 Olympics before joining the NHL for good in 1984-85.

17. Dave Ellett, who arrived in Toronto from the Winnipeg Jets in 1990, jumped to the Jets directly from Bowling Green University in 1984. Jamie Macoun jumped directly to the Calgary Flames from Ohio State in 1984.

18. Tracy Pratt, son of the great Babe Pratt, played 11 games with the Leafs during the 1976-77 season.

19. Tim Horton (3 First, 3 Second) and Borje Salming (1 First, 5 Second) are the leading Leaf All-Stars.

20. Frank "King" Clancy earned a berth on the NHL's First Team All-Stars in 1930-31, the first year the All-Star Team was formally selected.

21. Jim McKenny, who went from high school to the Toronto Marlboros, made his NHL debut during the 1965-66 season and retired in 1979 after being sold to Minnesota.

22. "Flash" Hollett, who played for the Leafs in 1933-34 and again from 1934 to 1936, scored 20 goals for Detroit in 1944-45. He played only 38 more games in the league after his milestone season.

23. Roger Jenkins was the first American-born defenceman, Borje Salming was the first European while Vitezslav Duris was the first player from a Communist country (Czechoslovakia) to man the blueline.

24. Jimmy Thomson, the Leafs captain in 1956-57, was exiled to the last place Chicago Black Hawks in 1957-58 – along with Detroit's Ted Lindsay – for their efforts in forming the first players union.

25. Pat Quinn, a blueliner for Toronto from 1968 to 1970, is currently the general manager of the Vancouver Canucks.

26. Marcel Pronovost, who survived the expansion draft to play with the Leafs until 1970, joined the Leafs from Detroit in 1965 in the trade that sent Andy Bathgate to the Red Wings.

27. Pierre Pilote spent the final year of his career with the Leafs, arriving in a trade for Jim Pappin, who compiled seven consecutive 20-goal seasons with the Hawks.

28. Gus Mortson compiled a league-leading 133 penalty minutes in 1946-47.

29. Jim Morrison wore numbers 3, 14, 21, 22, 24 in his 6½ seasons with the Leafs from January 9, 1952 to October 8, 1958.

30. Frank Mathers, who spent over 15 years as the coach of the AHL's Hershey Bears, was elected to the Hockey Hall of Fame in 1992. He played portions of three seasons with the Leafs from 1948 to 1952.

31. Bobby Baun, who scored the winning goal in overtime of game six during the 1964 finals, suffered a broken ankle in the third period of the game. After taping the ankle, he rejoined the team, returning to the ice in time to score the overtime winner. He also played the next game, a 4-0 Cup-winning victory for the Leafs. He spent the majority of the summer in a cast.

32. Fred Boimstruck (18 when the season started), Bob McGill (19), and Jim Benning (18) were the young defenders.

33. Joel Quenneville, who began his career with the Leafs in 1978-79, returned as an assistant coach with the St. John's Maple Leafs in 1991.

34. Alexander Godynyuk, who joined the Leafs from the Sokol Kiev team, was later traded to the Calgary Flames.

35. Drake Berehowsky was enjoying a fine 1992-93 campaign before a knee injury ended his season in the final regular- season game of the schedule.

36. Matt Martin, the Leafs' fourth selection in the 1989 Entry Draft, joined the St. John's Maple Leafs after the college season was completed in 1992-93.

37. Brad Marsh, the grinding defenceman who earned the fans' respect with his work ethic, was actually traded back to Toronto in June 1992 before being sent to Ottawa.

38. Janne Gronvall is expected to join the Leafs at their 1993-94 training camp in London, England.

39. Tim Horton (13 assists in 1962), Ian Turnbull (10 assists in 1978) and Todd Gill (10 assists in 1993).

40. Babe Pratt won the Hart Trophy in 1943-44 after setting an NHL record as the defenceman with the most assists (40) in a season.

Numerology

Match the following Leafs' defencemen with the only number they wore during their tenure with the team. Answers on page 124.

Al Arbour	11
Fred Boimistruck	2
Jim Dorey	23
Red Horner	26
Pat Quinn	3
Allan Stanley	8

③

Forwards Ho!

ALTHOUGH IT HAS BEEN NEARLY SIXTY YEARS SINCE the Maple Leafs have had an Art Ross Trophy winner as the league's scoring leader, the team has employed a number of outstanding forwards. From Conacher to Keon to Sittler to Gilmour, the team has had its share of prolific scorers. But the Leafs have never been built around a superstar. Team officials have preferred to acquire role players who can incorporate their talents into a team-orientated system.

However, numerous scoring leaders have played for the team through the years. Ace Bailey and Charlie Conacher each led the league in points in the team's formative years before Gordie Drillon won the team's last NHL scoring title in 1938, in only his second season in the league.

In 1947-48, Conn Smythe sent five players to Chicago to obtain Max Bentley, a two-time Art Ross winner, whose dipsy-doodling style and pin-point passes helped the Leafs to three Cups. In 1964, Punch Imlach sent five players to the New York Rangers to obtain the Rangers all-time leading scorer, Andy Bathgate. Although Bathgate's stay with the Leafs was brief, he led the team to the championship in 1964 and scored the Stanley Cup-winning goal.

One of the greatest forwards in franchise history was Frank Mahovlich, who led the team in goals for six consecutive seasons in the mid-1960s. When Mahovlich was traded to Detroit in 1968, the Leafs received Norm Ullman in return. The team's offensive leader for the next eight seasons, Ullman became the first player wearing a Leaf uniform to record his 1000th career point, in 1971.

Ullman's leadership and work ethic were passed on to Darryl Sittler, perhaps the finest player to wear the Leaf jersey in the last generation. Sittler was a natural talent who set numerous team records and holds the franchise record for career goals and points. Rick Vaive was the most prolific scorer on the Leaf teams of the 1980s, becoming the team's first 50-goal scorer and the only player in team history to score at least 50 goals in three straight campaigns.

One quality is evident in each of the great forwards who have played for the Leafs over the years. Each player has been exceptionally skilled as a leader, both on and off the ice. Conn Smythe once said that if he had to go to war with just one soldier, that man would be Ted Kennedy, because he was the bravest man he had ever seen play the game. It seems certain he would have applied the same accolades to Doug Gilmour, the current team's offensive sparkplug. When Gilmour signed his contract with the club, he refused all bonuses for individual achievement, insisting all extra money he received be determined by the team's performance. In 1992-93, Gilmour set new franchise records for assists and points in leading the team to one of the finest seasons in its history. In the play-offs, he established five new individual marks as the Leafs came within a single goal of reaching the Stanley Cup finals.

Questions

1. The first player signed by Conn Smythe after his group purchased the St. Pats franchise in February 1927 was an American-born forward who later captured the Calder Trophy with another team. What is his name and the name of the team he was with when he won the rookie of the year award?

2. This forward's tenure as the Leafs' general manager was so brief he is not even mentioned as being a GM in official team correspondence. Who is the player, why was he replaced and who succeeded him?

3. This forward is the only player in NHL history to score a hat-trick in overtime (In the early years, teams played a full 10-minute overtime period). Can you name this sudden-death sniper?

4. This stylish centre won the gold medal in pole-vaulting at the 1934 British Empire Games and represented Canada at the Berlin Olympics in 1936. Who was this multi-talented performer?

5. This centreman from Winnipeg was the first NHLer

to wear a moustache. Name the whiskered face-off artist.

6. In 1943-44, this forward set an NHL record by scoring his first NHL goal only 15 seconds into his first NHL game. Name this quick-starter.

7. During the 1992-93 season, this Leaf forward tied a team record that had stood for 49 years. What was the record and who tied it?

8. In 1970, the Leafs traded one of their all-time greats to the Los Angeles Kings. Can you name the future Hall of Famer the Leafs sent to Hollywood and the player they received in return?

9. The longest-serving Maple Leaf began his career during the 1949-50 season. Can you name this elder statesman?

10. In 1976, Darryl Sittler had the finest season of his career, highlighted by three outstanding achievements. Can you recall his three trips to immortality?

11. Can you name the former Leaf who became the first Russian-born player to earn a berth in the Hockey Hall of Fame?

12. This Maple Leaf farmhand who started his career with the New York Rangers was the first NHL player to be killed in the Second World War. Can you name this hero?

13. This left-winger, a member of the Leafs' Cup-winning team in 1948, left professional hockey to become a priest. He later formed the famous "Flying Fathers" hockey team. Can you name him?

14. Who was the only Maple Leaf player to wear number 99?

15. Who holds the Maple Leafs record for most seasons with MORE than 20 goals scored?

16. This popular Leaf forward scored at least 20 goals for five different NHL teams. Can you name this entertaining individual and the teams he reached the milestone with?

17. This speedy forward scored his first NHL goal in his first NHL game, a 1988 playoff encounter with Detroit. Name him.

18. Name the first Leaf to elected to the NHL's All-Rookie Team.

19. I led the Leafs and the entire NHL in shorthanded goals one year and was cut from the Leafs during training camp the following season. Who am I?

20. This former Leaf forward was the first player in NHL history to lead three different teams in scoring in three consecutive seasons. Can you name this travelling scoring machine?

21. This forward, who started his career with the Leafs in the mid-1970s, set a record for goals in the minor leagues. Can you name this productive prodigy?

22. This Leaf winger was originally selected by the Calgary Flames in the entry draft with a pick they originally acquired from the Leafs. Name the forward.

23. Name the only Leaf forward since the universal draft was introduced in 1969 to be chosen directly out of high school and play for Toronto.

24. What number did Frank Mahovlich wear when he made his professional debut with the Leafs in March 1957?

25. Name the only member of the 1992-93 Toronto Maple Leafs to have scored a Stanley Cup-winning goal.

26. This right-winger was better known for his play on the gridiron than his performance on the ice. Name this two-sport star and the football team that made him famous.

27. This forward played only three games for the Maple Leafs in his entire career, but he has his name on the Stanley Cup as a member of the 1967 team. Who was the fortunate forward?

28. Name the only two players to record their 1000th career point while playing with the Maple Leafs.

29. This player was one of the most productive goal scorers of the 1920s, but was traded before Toronto became the Maple Leafs. He did, however, finish his career with the Leafs. Name him and the year he played as a Maple Leaf.

30. In the 1964 semi-finals, the Leafs were tied with the Montreal Canadiens at three games apiece. This classy player single-handedly won the series by scoring one short-handed goal, one even strength goal, and one empty-net goal in the Leafs 3-1 victory. Name him.

31. Name the only Leaf player to lead the league in shots on goal since the category was introduced in 1968. How many shots did he take and in what year did he record this franchise first?

32. Name the Leaf farmhand who won four Stanley Cup rings in the 1980s but didn't play a game in the NHL in 1992-93.

33. Name the last Leaf forward to earn a spot on the NHL's First Team All-Stars and the year he earned the honour.

34. This lanky left-winger became the first player in NHL

history to score at least 25 goals for two teams in the same season. Do you know his name and the number of goals he scored?

35. Name the only Leaf winger to "officially" serve as the team's general manager when his playing days were over.

36. This former Leaf forward led the WHA in scoring in the league's second year of operation. Name him.

37. Only one player in NHL history has won more than six Stanley Cup rings without playing for the Montreal Canadiens. He was a playmaking centre for the Leafs who was a crowd favourite. Can you identify him?

38. The first Newfoundlander to play in the NHL started his career as a centre with the Maple Leafs. Name him.

39. One of the most travelled veterans in NHL history, this centre played on eight NHL teams, including the Leafs. In 1978-79, he finished third in goals scored for the club. Who was he?

Answers

1. Carl Voss, a native of Chelsea, Massachusetts, played 12 games for the Leafs and 10 games with the New York Rangers before winning the Calder Trophy with Detroit in 1932-33, five years after he made his NHL debut with Toronto in February 1927.

2. Howie Meeker served as the Leafs' GM for five months in between the 1956-57 and 1957-58 seasons. He was relieved of his duties before ever managing

a game during the season by Stafford Smythe, who told the press that Meeker didn't have the experience to be a G.M. in the NHL. The post was left vacant for the 1957-58 season while the "Silver Seven" (Mara, Bassett, Amell, Smythe, Gardiner, Hatch, and Ballard) ran the team. Punch Imalch won the job three months into the 1958-59 campaign.

3. Ken Doraty, who scored only nine goals all season in 1933-34, scored three of them in the Leafs' 7-4 overtime victory over the Ottawa Senators on January 16, 1934.

4. Syl Apps actually joined the Leafs after the 1936 Olympics for a western Canada exhibition tour with the Chicago Black Hawks.

5. Andy Blair, a defensive specialist for eight seasons, was famous for his "shadowed upper lip."

6. Gus Bodnar, who captured the Calder Trophy in 1944, had his finest NHL season as a rookie, recording 62 points. He never collected more than 45 for the rest of his 12 year career.

7. Doug Gilmour registered six assists against the Minnesota North Stars on February 13, 1993, tying Babe Pratt's mark established on January 9, 1944.

8. The Leafs traded Bob Pulford to the Los Angeles Kings on September 3, 1970 in return for Garry Monahan. Monahan, who spent four full seasons with the Leafs before being dealt to Vancouver, finished his career with Toronto in 1978-79.

9. George Armstrong spent his entire career with the Leafs, appearing in 1,187 games.

10. In 1976, Sittler set an NHL record with 10 points in a game; tied an NHL record with five goals in a single

playoff game; and scored the winning goal for Team Canada in the inaugural Canada Cup tournament.

11. Dave "Sweeney" Schriner, who joined the Leafs from the New York Americans in 1939, was born in Saratov, Russia, and immigrated to Canada at the age of eight months.

12. Dudley "Red" Garrett's memory is immortalized by the American Hockey League, which awards the Dudley "Red" Garrett Memorial Trophy to the league's best rookie.

13. Les Costello played only a handful of games in the NHL before forming the "Flying Fathers," who played thousands of games for charity.

14. Wilf Paiement, who joined the Leafs in the Lanny McDonald trade, wore number 99 in 1979-80, the first year that Wayne Gretzky wore the number in the NHL.

15. Ron Ellis scored more than 20 goals in 11 of his 16 years wearing the Maple Leafs uniform.

16. Eddie Shack scored 20 or more goals in a season for, respectively, Toronto, Boston, Los Angeles, Buffalo, and Pittsburgh.

17. Daniel Marois scored his first NHL goal in Detroit's 6-2 victory over Toronto in the 1988 Norris Division semi-final.

18. Dangerous Dan Daoust, who was traded to the Leafs in December 1982 from the Montreal Canadiens, earned the centre's spot on the NHL's first All-Rookie Team in 1983.

19. Dave "Sniper" Reid scored eight short-handed goals in the 1989-90 season but was released during training camp. He later signed with Boston.

20. Vincent Damphousse led the Leafs in scoring 1991, the Edmonton Oilers in scoring in 1992, and the Montreal Canadiens in scoring in 1993.

21. Bruce Boudreau, who was the Leafs' third selection in 1975 Amateur Draft, scored 548 goals in the CHL, AHL, NAHL, and IHL.

22. Kent Manderville, selected by Calgary in the second round of the 1989 Entry Draft with a pick they acquired in the Rob Ramage trade, was dealt to Toronto in January 1992.

23. Paul Higgins, chosen 200th out of Toronto High School in 1980, holds the dubious record of playing 25 games over two seasons without compiling any points and registering only one shot on goal. He did, however, collect 152 penalty minutes.

24. The "Big M" wore number 26 when he had a three-game trial with the Leafs in 1957.

25. Doug Gilmour scored the Cup-winner for the Calgary Flames against the Montreal Canadiens at 11:02 of the third period in game six of the 1989 finals.

26. Gerry James played portions of five seasons with the Leafs but was best known as a running back for the Winnipeg Blue Bombers of the Canadian Football League (CFL).

27. Milan Marcetta played three games for Toronto during the 1967 finals against Montreal, enough to earn him a spot on the Stanley Cup.

28. Norm Ullman (October 16, 1971, against New York Rangers) and Glenn Anderson (February 22, 1993, against Vancouver) are the only two players to register point #1000 while playing with the Leafs.

29. Babe Dye, the St. Pats' finest player, led or tied for the

NHL lead in goals three times. He returned to Toronto to finish his career in 1930-31.

30. Dave Keon, in the game of a lifetime, fired the hat-trick to propel the Leafs into the finals.

31. Darryl Sittler led the NHL with 311 shots on goal in 1978, one more than Montreal's Jacques Lemaire.

32. Kevin McClelland, who won four Cups with the Oilers in the 1980s, spent the entire 1992-93 season with the St. John's Maple Leafs.

33. Frank Mahovlich was selected as the NHL's top left-winger in 1962-63 when he scored 36 goals.

34. Dave Andreychuk scored 29 goals for Buffalo and 25 goals for Toronto for a total of 54 during the 1992-93 season.

35. Floyd Smith, who arrived in Toronto in the Frank Mahovlich trade, served as GM from 1989 to 1991.

36. Mike Walton, who spent portions of six seasons with the Leafs, jumped from the Boston Bruins to the WHA's Minnesota Fighting Saints and led the WHA in points with 117 in 1973-74.

37. Red Kelly won four Cups with Toronto and four Cups with Detroit.

38. Alex Faulkner, a native of Bishops Falls, Newfoundland, started his career with the Leafs during the 1961-62 season.

39. Walt McKechnie, who scored 25 goals for the Leafs in 1978-79, played 954 regular-season games but only 15 playoff games in his 16-year NHL career.

Famous Lines

Match the names of these famous Leaf forward lines with their members. Answers on page 125.

1. The Hound Line
2. The Kid Line
3. The Rocks
4. The Flying Forts
5. The "New" Kid Line
6. The DAD Line
7. The SAW Line
8. The KSS Line
9. The MAD Line

a. Gus Bodnar, Gaye Stewart, Bud Poile
b. Ted Kennedy, Sid Smith, Tod Sloan
c. Russ Courtnall, Gary Leeman, Wendel Clark
d. Gary Edmundson, Gerry James, Johnny Wilson
e. Tod Sloan, George Armstrong, Harry Watson
f. Nick Metz, Syl Apps, Gordie Drillon
g. Joe Primeau, Charlie Conacher, Busher Jackson
h. Bob Davidson, Syl Apps, Gordie Drillon
i. Darryl Sittler, Rick Kehoe, Denis Dupere

Through the Years

THROUGHOUT THE STORIED HISTORY OF THE TOR-
onto Maple Leaf franchise, some of the game's greatest
characters have pulled on the team's blue and white jersey. From the days of Conn Smythe through the Ballard
years, the Leafs have always had a place for the game's
eccentrics, players who could perform on the ice and
were often a touch off the wall outside the rink.

The early Leaf teams included a certified pharmacist
in Hap Day, a colourful all-round athlete who played
baseball, football, rugby, and hockey in Charlie
Conacher, and a distinguished track star who won a gold
medal at the British Empire Games in Syl Apps. Added to
this mix was Andy Blair, a defensive forward renowned
for his elegant manners and stylish moustache. He was
also known for carrying a handkerchief tucked up the
sleeve of his jersey, which was constantly being stolen by

opposing forwards eager to get under the passive Blair's scalp.

Of course, the greatest character of them all was Francis "King" Clancy, the Irish leprechaun with the gift of gab. One of his most notorious achievements involved knocking Eddie Shore out of a pivotal playoff game, not with a resounding body check, but with his clever wit. In game two of the 1936 quarter-finals, with the Bruins leading the two-game total-goal series 4-3, Clancy stepped alongside Shore in the faceoff circle and mentioned that he thought the Bruins were the recipients of a bad call by referee Odie Cleghorn and that the third Leaf goal surely shouldn't have counted. The King then suggested that Shore take up a verbal debate with Cleghorn and get that obvious miscarriage of justice corrected. For some reason Shore, who had already been in the penalty box for a pair of Leaf goals and was in a surly mood, listened to Clancy's advice and gave referee Cleghorn an earful. When Cleghorn refused to listen, Shore shot the puck at him and earned a ten-minute stay in the sin-bin. With the Bruins' best defender out of action, the Leafs scored three quick goals to win the game and the series

Other legendary Leaf moments include the great weight debate or Turk Broda's "Battle of the Bulge." In 1950-51, Conn Smythe suspended Turk Broda for being overweight, prompting thousands of fans to send in diet plans, and the newspapers to hold a daily "fat count." When Broda was down to the required weight, he returned to the nets and recorded a shutout in his first game back

Other characters to don the Maple Leaf include Bill

Ezinicki, who held out every year to get some extra golf-ing in, and Carl Brewer, who held out just to make Punch Imlach mad. Eddie Shack, a true on-ice entertainer who had a hit song penned in his honour, had a bowlegged skating style that endeared him to the Gardens faithful for years. Tiger Williams shot a bear with a bow and arrow and sent the hide to Harold Ballard, who proudly displayed it in his office. Ballard, perhaps the most colourful owner in recent history, set his hand and foot prints in the cement under the centre-ice dot in Maple Leaf Gardens. The imprints eventually had to be filled in because the ice kept collapsing in that area. Al Iafrate rode a Harley Davidson motorcycle to practice, which doesn't seem as odd now since it happens to be coach Pat Burns' favoured mode of transportation as well.

Questions

1. Many former Maple Leafs have been active – and successful – in politics. Can you name four former players whose off-ice oratorical skills won them political prestige either federally or provincially?
2. Since 1969, four players who were selected first over-all in the amateur or entry draft have played for the Leafs. Name the quartet and the teams that originally selected them.
3. Who was the last player from the 1967 Stanley Cup-winning team to retire and what team was he with when he finally hung up the blades?
4. Name the 11 men to score Stanley Cup-winning

goals for the Toronto Maple Leafs and supply the years in which they scored them.

5. The only player to be selected in the both 1967 and 1979 expansion drafts played briefly for the Leafs in the mid-1970s. Can you recall who this player was?

6. This rough 'n' ready Maple Leaf became a successful pro golfer when his playing days were over. Can you remember this forward who traded pucks for putts in the 1950s?

7. This forward, who finished his career in Toronto, scored one of the most famous goals in the history of the Los Angeles Kings franchise, an overtime winner that completed a five-goal comeback against Edmonton in game three of the 1982 playoffs. Name him.

8. This classy centre's father and uncle played for the Leafs in the late 1950s. Can you trace his heritage and name him, his father, and his uncle?

9. This opportunistic marksman established himself as a playoff hero in 1939 as a member of the Boston Bruins by scoring three overtime goals in the same series. He finished his career as a Leaf, helping Toronto win the Cup in 1945. Who is he?

10. This former Leaf (1930-31) is the only player in the history of the NHL to score a goal in his one and only game. This is a tough one, but can you name him?

11. This player, one of the greatest performers in Detroit Red Wings' history, spent part of the 1931-32 season with the Leafs. Name him.

12. After he became assistant general manager of the Toronto Maple Leafs in 1957, Punch Imlach

attempted to sign two outstanding minor-league stars. One, Johnny Bower, went on to be one of the NHL's greatest goaltenders. The other player, who went on to become the highest scorer in minor-league history, decided not to return to the NHL and remained in the minors. Can you name him?

13. This one-time Leaf goaltender was the first player to win three Rookie of the Year awards in three different leagues. Can you can remember this renowned rookie and the teams he won the freshmen award with?

14. This member of the Buffalo Sabres' famed "French Connection" began and ended his career with Toronto. Name him and the years that bracketed his stay with the most famous forward unit of the 1970s.

15. This centre, who played for the Leafs in 1962-63, was the last Black Hawk to wear the number 9 before Bobby Hull. Who was he?

16. The Leafs were the first NHL team to use three goal-tenders in one game. Can you name the three goalies and the year that this odd turn of events took place?

17. In a March 1966 game against Chicago, a Leafs defenceman was suspended for two games for taking a swing at linesman John D'Amico. Can you name the rambunctious rearguard?

18. One of Conn Smythe's stranger rules prohibited players from getting married during the season. In 1951, one young Leaf forward broke the rule and was immediately banished to the minors. Name the guilty groom.

19. Who was the first black athlete to play for the Toronto

Maple Leafs, and in what year did he make his debut with the club?

20. This player, who started his career with Toronto during the 1975-76 season before being traded to Los Angeles in 1978, was killed in a motor-vehicle accident in 1979. Can you name him?

21. In game two of the Toronto-New York Rangers quarter-finals in 1971, Leaf goaltender Jacques Plante had to be replaced by Bernie Parent because of strange circumstances. What were they?

22. Can you remember the forward whom Harold Ballard described as being able to "go into a corner with half a dozen eggs in his pocket and not break one"?

23. During his 15-year career with the Leafs, Dave Keon collected only one major penalty, in a game against Boston toward the end of the 1973-74 schedule. Can you name the antagonist who enticed the normally calm Keon into a brief display of fisticuffs?

24. When did Maple Leaf Gardens open and who provided the Leafs' opposition on opening night?

25. Prior to playing at the Gardens, where did the Leafs play their home games?

26. Who was the last Leaf player to win the J.P. Bickell Cup as the team's MVP?

27. In 1936, the Leafs and Chicago Black Hawks played a cross-Canada post-season exhibition series for the Totem Trophy. Two future Leaf stars made their debut in this series. Name them.

28. Which Leaf won the Molson Cup award for the 1990-91 season?

29. Who was the first Leaf to record a hat-trick?

30. Who was the first Leaf to score a penalty-shot goal?

31. In 1985-86, the Leafs reached the Divisional Finals for the first time since the current playoff format was established. After defeating the Blackhawks, the Leafs lost in seven games to St. Louis, including a 4-3 overtime defeat in the pivotal game five. Who scored the overtime winner for the Blues?

32. This former Leafs goaltender surrendered Bobby Hull's record-breaking 51st goal on March 12, 1966. Name him and the year(s) he wore the blue and white.

33. This well-travelled defenceman played for eight NHL teams and two WHA teams, winning the Cup with Detroit, Toronto, and Montreal. Name him.

34. In 1964, Johnny Bower had a hit record on the Christmas pop charts. Name the tune and the name of Bower's band.

35. During the building of Maple Leaf Gardens, Smythe and his financiers ran out of cash. They developed an intriguing idea to get the work finished in time for the 1931-32 season. What was the idea, and who was the man responsible for pulling it off?

36. On February 14, 1934, the first All-Star Game was played as a benefit for the family of Ace Bailey, the injured Maple Leaf star. It was a game between Toronto and a team of All-Stars. The Leafs had a special name that evening. What were they known as for this match and what was the final score?

37. Who was the Leafs' main scout during the formative years of the franchise, responsible for scouring the western provinces for talent?

38. In 1940-41, the Leafs placed three players on the

NHL's First All-Star Team. Can you recall their names?

39. This NHL coach, a former Leafs defenceman in his playing days, was the first person to win the Jack Adams Award as the NHL's coach of the year with two different teams. Who is he?

Answers

1. Red Kelly (Federal, York West), Bucko McDonald (Federal, Parry Sound), Syl Apps (Provincial, Kingston), and Howie Meeker (Federal, Kitchener-Waterloo).

2. Billy Harris, selected first overall by the New York Islanders in the 1972 Amateur Draft, played for Toronto from 1981 to 1984. Dale McCourt, selected first overall by Detroit in the 1977 Amateur Draft, played for the Leafs during the 1983-84 season. Rob Ramage, selected first overall by the Colorado Rockies in 1979 spent 160 games with the Leafs from 1989 to 1991. And, of course, Wendel Clark, taken by Toronto first overall in the 1985 Entry Draft, has played for Toronto from 1985 to the present day.

3. Dave Keon retired following the 1981-82 season. After leaving the Leafs in 1975, he played with Minnesota, Indianapolis, and New England of the WHA. He spent his last three NHL seasons with the Hartford Whalers.

4. Ace Bailey (1932), Pete Langelle (1942), Babe Pratt (1945), Ted Kennedy (1947), Harry Watson (1948), Cal Gardner (1949), Bill Barilko (1951), Dick Duff

(1962), Eddie Shack (1963), Andy Bathgate (1964), Jim Pappin (1967).

5. Doug Favell, who played for Toronto from 1973 to 1976, was selected by Philadelphia from Boston in the 1967 expansion draft and by Edmonton off the roster of the Colorado Rockies in the 1979 expansion draft.

6. Wild Bill Ezinicki joined the PGA Tour in the mid-1950s and won a number of tournaments including the Bob Hope Classic.

7. Daryl Evans scored the overtime winner for the Kings and finished his career in the Leafs' system.

8. John Cullen joined the Leafs in December 1992, completing the family circle that included father Barry (1955-1959) and uncle Brian (1954-1959). Another Cullen, uncle Ray, played with four NHL teams, including the Rangers and North Stars, from 1965-71.

9. The overtime hero was Mel "Sudden Death" Hill, who scored the only three overtime goals of his career in the Boston-New York Rangers semi-final of 1939.

10. Roland (Rolly) Huard scored a goal in his only appearance in an NHL uniform during the 1930-31 season.

11. Hall of Famer Syd Howe played on four different teams before settling in with the Detroit Red Wings in 1934-35. When the Ottawa Senators took a leave of absence for the 1931-32 season, Howe was loaned to the Leafs.

12. Guyle Fielder, who played for Chicago, Detroit, and Boston in the NHL, was the most prolific scorer in minor-league history, compiling 1,929 regular

season and 108 playoff points from 1950 to 1973 in the PCHL, AHL, and WHL.

13. Terry Sawchuk won the USHL rookie award with the Omaha Knights in 1948, the AHL rookie award with the Indianapolis Caps in 1949, and the Calder Trophy with Detroit as the NHL's best freshman in 1951.

14. René Robert, who was claimed by the Buffalo Sabres in the 1971 expansion draft, played five games for the Leafs in 1970-71. He returned to the Leafs in 1981 and finished his career as a Maple Leaf.

15. Bronco Horvath wore number 9 in 1961-62, his only season with the Black Hawks. Hull, who started his career wearing number 16, switched to number 7 before donning the number 9 jersey in 1962-63. Hull stated he made the switch out of respect for Gordie Howe.

16. On April 3, 1966, in a 3-3 tie against the Detroit Red Wings, Johnny Bower (first period), Terry Sawchuk (second period), and Bruce Gamble (third period) alternated in nets for the Leafs.

17. Defenceman Kent Douglas, who had already been involved in a couple of altercations, took on Chicago's Doug Mohns and linesman D'Amico in the third period of the Leafs' 4-2 win, earning a two-game stay on the sidelines.

18. Johnny "Goose" McCormack got married in January 1951, earning him a honeymoon in Pittsburgh with the Leafs farm team, the Hornets. Sold to Montreal in September 1951, he played on the Habs' Stanley Cup-winning team in 1953 before finishing his career in Chicago.

19. Val James, who appeared briefly with the Leafs

during the 1986-87 season, started his career with the Buffalo Sabres in 1981.

20. Scott Garland was killed in a car accident near Montreal in June 1979. He recorded 29 points in 69 games for the Leafs in 1976-77.

21. In the third period, Ranger forward Vic Hadfield grabbed Plante's mask and tossed it into the crowd. Fans at Madison Square Garden would not return it. Plante had only one mask with him, and Parent was forced to enter the game, a 4-1 victory for the Leafs.

22. Inge Hammarstrom, one of two Swedish imports signed by the Leafs in 1972, actually collected two five-minute majors in his brief career in Toronto.

23. Gregg Sheppard, who never collected more than 49 penalty minutes in a season, was the unlikely combatant who drew a five minute-major out of Keon. It was the first major penalty in Sheppard's career as well.

24. The Gardens opened on November 12, 1931, with the Chicago Black Hawks playing the Leafs. Chicago squeezed by the Buds 2-1 to spoil an otherwise outstanding evening.

25. From 1927 to 1931, the Leafs played their home games at the Mutual Street Arena, which was turned into a bowling alley and a curling and roller-skating rink in its final years.

26. Mike Palmateer won the J.P. Bickell Cup in 1979 and the trophy has not been awarded since.

27. Syl Apps and Gordie Drillon both made their debuts in the Totem Trophy series. Apps, who just returned from the Olympics, played for the Leafs. Interest-

ingly, Drillon played for the Hawks, who were short of players in the post-season exhibition set.

28. Goaltender Peter Ing, who was traded in September 1991, won the annual award for compiling the most three-star selections during the season.

29. Hap Day was the first Leaf to score three goals in a game, notching a hat-trick on January 17, 1928.

30. Charlie Conacher, who took the first four penalty shots in franchise history, finally connected on his fourth try, firing a penalty shot behind New York Americans goalie Roy Worters in a 3-0 Leafs victory on February 8, 1936.

31. Mark Reeds scored the winning goal for the Blues, the only overtime goal of his career and the last play-off goal he would score.

32. Cesare Maniago, who appeared in seven games during the 1960-61 season, was playing for the Rangers when Bobby Hull broke the record for goals in a single season.

33. Larry Hillman, who started his career in Detroit, before moving on to Boston, Toronto, Minnesota, Montreal, Philadelphia, Los Angeles, and Buffalo, played two seasons with brother Wayne in Philadelphia.

34. Bower's hit, which was recorded the same night as the "Great Blackout" power shortage on the eastern U.S. seaboard, was called "Honky, the Christmas Goose." The band was logically called the "Rinky Dinks."

35. In lieu of cash, Smythe offered the workers shares of stock in the new Gardens. Although the men were

sceptical at first, Frank Selke, a leading voice in the Electricians Union, convinced the builders that the stock was better than money. He was proved right, and the Gardens was finished in time.

36. The Leafs were known as the "Aces" for this game between them and a group of NHL All-Stars. The "Aces" defeated the Stars 6-2.

37. George "Squib" Walker was the Leafs major talent scout, bringing in players such as Buzz Boll, Charlie Sands, Gus Mortson, and Gaye Stewart.

38. Turk Broda (goal), Wally Stanowski (defence), and Sweeney Schriner (left wing) all had outstanding seasons for the Leafs and were voted to the league's First All-Star Team.

39. Pat Quinn, who earned coach of the year honours with Philadelphia and Vancouver, never played in the NHL until the Leafs purchased him from the St. Louis Blues in 1968.

Name the Real Names

Match the nicknames of the following Maple Leaf forwards with the names in the right column. Answers on page 125.

1.	"Shakey"	a.	Elwyn Romnes
2.	"The Big Bomber"	b.	Frank Mahovlich
3.	"Spinner"	c.	Charlie Conacher
4.	"The Entertainer"	d.	Joe Klukay
5.	"Motor City Smitty"	e.	Eddie Shack
6.	"Squidly"	f.	Frank Boll
7.	"Killer"	g.	Mel Hill
8.	"Bomber"	h.	Harold Cotton
9.	"Ozzy"	i.	Blaine Stoughton
10.	"Busher"	j.	Leonard Kelly
11.	"Stemmer"	k.	Dave Schriner
12.	"The Big M"	l.	Brad Smith
13.	"Red"	m.	Peter Stemkowski
14.	"The Chief"	n.	Ken Baumgartner
15.	"Bingo"	o.	Wally Stanowski
16.	"Buzz"	p.	Garry Edmundson
17.	"Duke of Paducah"	q.	Rudy Kampman
18.	"Sudden Death"	r.	Mark Osborne
19.	"Cowboy"	s.	Rick Vaive
20.	"Baldy"	t.	Bill Fleet
21.	"Duke"	u.	Brian Spencer
22.	"Doc"	v.	Mike Walton
23.	"Sweeney"	w.	Doug Gilmour
24.	"The Whirling Dervish"	x.	Harvey Jackson
25.	"Stash"	y.	George Armstrong

Coaches, Captains, and the King

SOME OF THE NHL'S GREATEST COACHES HAVE STOOD behind the bench at Maple Leaf Gardens. Indeed, six Leaf coaches have earned a berth in the Hockey Hall of Fame, including Punch Imlach, Dick Irvin, King Clancy, and Hap Day. Clancy never coached the Leafs to a Stanley Cup victory, but he was the team's "good-will ambassador" until his death in 1986. Once Conn Smythe stopped him and asked, "King, what is it you do around here?" Clancy replied, "Well, not much of anything, Mr. Smythe." Smythe paused, then said, "Well, keep it up, you're doing a great job."

Dick Irvin, the first man to coach three different teams to the Stanley Cup finals, led the Leafs into the finals on seven occasions, winning the championship in 1932. His successor, Hap Day, piloted the Leafs into the winner's circle five times, including a trifecta of titles from 1947 to 1949. Although both of these perceptive hockey men were excellent coaches, they were inducted into the Hall of Fame as players. The trend in the formative years of the NHL was to hire former NHL players as coaches. The Leafs broke that tradition when they hired Punch Imlach in 1958. Imlach was a fine minor-league player who never made it to the show, but his knowledge of the game and his ability to deliver that knowledge to his players made him one of the game's finest tacticians. His stay with the Leafs from 1958-1969 produced four Stanley Cup titles and earned him a spot on the Hockey Hall of Fame's honour roll as a builder.

Even those coaches who had only limited success in Toronto went on to have outstanding coaching careers in other arenas. Billy Reay's stay in Toronto was brief, but he went on to lead the Chicago Blackhawks from 1963 to 1976. Roger Neilson spent only two campaigns as the Leafs' coach, but he has gone on to become one of the league's finest strategists, constantly in demand by rebuilding clubs.

The current Leaf squad is coached by one of hockey's finest talents and a man who never played professional hockey. Pat Burns became the first Leaf coach to earn the Jack Adams Award as coach of the year in 1992-93, leading the team to its highest point total in franchise history. Burns, who earned similar accolades with the Montreal Canadiens, is a no-nonsense competitor whose well-defined defensive system paid instant dividends for the Maple Leafs.

The role of the captain on a team is to insure that the coaches orders are being followed on the ice and to act as a liaison between the coaching staff and the on-ice officials. The captain is also the off-ice leader, controlling the dressing room and setting the emotional tempo of the game. The Leafs' first captain, Hap Day, was also one of the franchise's best coaches. Ted Kennedy, who replaced Syl Apps in 1948, is one of the club's best remembered captains, a player who constantly led by example. George Armstrong, Dave Keon, and Darryl Sittler followed in that same mold, unselfish on the ice and compassionate leaders in the dressing room. Wendel Clark, the team's present captain, is a throwback to another generation, a hard-hitting dynamo on the ice and a vocal disciplinarian outside the rink. In today's NHL, the role of the captain has become largely ceremonial. However, for successful franchises, the captain is a natural extension of the coach, and their combined talents can raise a club above its rivals.

Questions

1. Who was the first man to win the "Triple Crown" as a coach, leading his teams to the Stanley Cup, Allan Cup, and Memorial Cup championships?
2. This former Leaf captain coached the Toronto Marlboros to the Memorial Cup in 1973 and 1975. Name him.
3. Everyone knows that Conn Smythe purchased King Clancy from the Ottawa Senators for $35,000, an unheard-of price during the Depression. Smythe also sent two players to the Senators. Name them.
4. Name the man whom Dick Irvin replaced as coach five games into the 1931-32 season.
5. Who captained the Leafs to the Stanley Cup in 1945?

6. King Clancy was the first player in Stanley Cup history to play defence, forward, and goal in the same game. When did the King accomplish this trifecta?

7. Five different men stood behind the bench for the Leafs from 1979-80 to 1980-81. Name this quintet of coaches.

8. Two men have served as captain of the Leafs twice. Who were they and why did each give up his captaincy in the first place?

9. Although King Clancy didn't coach the Leafs to the Stanley Cup, he did coach a team to a championship. Can you name the team, the league, and the year in which the King was king?

10. Keeping it in the family: Incredibly, 13 former players have coached the Maple Leafs. Can you name them all?

11. Rick Vaive served as the Leafs' captain from 1981 to 1986 before being asked to step down. Why was he asked to remove the "C"?

12. In 1949, King Clancy was given a prestigious position by the NHL, but he resigned after only one week to take a coaching job. What job did he resign from and what team did he sign on to coach?

13. Darryl Sittler wrote an unfortunate chapter in Leafs history when he abruptly quit as captain before a game. What were the circumstances behind Sittler's decision?

14. One of the King's proudest moments came when he pinch-hit for an exhausted Punch Imlach and stepped behind the bench while Imlach rested in hospital. When did this take place and what was the King's record during his stint?

15. Three former Leaf coaches also piloted teams in the WHA. Who were the coaches and what teams did they lead in the rival league?

16. Two former Leaf captains also served in that capacity for other NHL squads. Name this dependable duo and the other teams they each captained?

17. What was the first team to hire King Clancy as a coach after he retired in 1936?

18. Who did Punch Imlach replace as coach when he came aboard in 1958?

19. Two former Leaf captains have won the Lady Byng Trophy twice. Name this gentlemanly pair and the years they won the award.

20. King Clancy returned behind the Leafs' bench in 1972 as an emergency replacement for John McLellan. What was the King's record and what award did he receive at the end of his term?

21. In the Leafs' formative days, Conn Smythe served as the teams manager-coach, but in the first days after purchasing the club, he was too busy with his Toronto Varsity senior team to manage the new Leafs. Who filled Smythe's shoes from February 14, 1927 to the end of the season?

22. Who was the first Leafs captain to reach the 200-goal plateau?

23. What goaltender surrendered King Clancy's first NHL goal?

24. What former Leafs coach won the Jack Adams Trophy as the NHL's coach of the year?

25. Who was the Leafs captain from 1986 to 1989?

26. To raise the money to buy King Clancy, Conn Smythe had to do some fancy wheeling and dealing, on the

ice and off. He raised the final $10,000 he needed at the racetrack with a well-placed purse on the ponies. Can you name the horse that came in for Smythe and brought home Clancy?

27. Although he never coached the Leafs, this astute hockey mind made most of the major decisions for the club during the war years, in which Toronto won the Cup in 1942 and 1945. Who was he?

28. Who was the first Leafs captain to actually wear a "C" on his uniform?

29. Who replaced King Clancy on the Leafs blueline when the King retired six games into the 1936-37 season?

Answers

1. Gentleman Joe Primeau coached the Toronto St. Michaels to the Memorial Cup (1945, 1948), the Toronto Marlboro seniors to the Allan Cup (1950), and the Toronto Maple Leafs to the Stanley Cup (1951).

2. George Armstrong, the longest-serving Leaf in franchise history, had a successful coaching reign with the Marlies, winning a pair of national championships.

3. Smythe sent Art Smith and Eric Pettinger to the Senators. Although both players saw limited action in 1930-31 season with Ottawa, neither played in the NHL after his one-season stay in the nation's capital.

4. Art Duncan, who led the Leafs to a 21-13-8 mark in

1930-31, was fired after Toronto opened the 1931-32 season with five consecutive losses.

5. Bob Davidson, who spent his entire 13-year career with the Leafs, served as the team captain from 1943 to 1945.

6. The King, a natural defenceman, was forced to take a few shifts at centre and on the wing during a Cup challenge match against Edmonton on March 29, 1923. The Senators, who were playing the game with only one sub, also had Clancy take a shift in nets when goaltender Clint Benedict was penalized for slashing. It was only the seventh playoff game in Clancy's young career.

7. After firing Roger Neilson following the 1978-79 season, Harold Ballard had Dick Duff, Punch Imlach, Floyd Smith, Joe Crozier, and Mike Nykoluk take turns coaching the team over the next two seasons.

8. Syl Apps served as captain from 1940-41 to 1942-43 and from 1945-46 to 1947-48. He resigned as captain to serve in the Armed Forces in the Second World War. Ted Kennedy, who was the Leafs' captain from 1948-49 to 1954-55, once again served as captain in 1956-57 when he returned to the team after 18 months of retirement.

9. The King coached the Pittsburgh Hornets, the Leafs' number-one farm team, to the AHL's Calder Cup championship in 1952.

10. Art Duncan, Hap Day, Joe Primeau, King Clancy, Howie Meeker, John McLellan, Red Kelly, Floyd Smith, Dick Duff, Joe Crozier, Mike Nykoluk, Dan Maloney, and George Armstrong have all coached the Leafs.

11. Vaive slept in and missed a mandatory 7:15 a.m. team practice on February 22, 1986. He was ordered to surrender his captaincy by Harold Ballard.

12. Clancy was named as the NHL's Referee-in-Chief in June 1949, but he resigned to coach the Cincinnati Mohawks in the AHL.

13. Sittler was protesting the trade that sent Lanny McDonald to the Colorado Rockies on December 29, 1979. He ripped the captain's "C" off his jersey before the Leafs' next game.

14. The King led the Leafs to a 7-1-2 mark during the 1966-67 season. Clancy's easy going manner behind the bench was just the tonic the Leafs needed, and the team rattled off a long unbeaten streak.

15. John Brophy, Joe Crozier, and Floyd Smith all coached in the WHA. Brophy, who coached the Leafs from 1986-87 to December 1988, was the last coach of the WHA's Birmingham Bulls in 1978-79. Crozier coached the Vancouver Blazers (1974-75) and the Calgary Cowboys (1975-77) while Floyd Smith piloted the Cincinnati Stingers (1978-79).

16. Dave Keon, who captained the Leafs from 1969 to 1975, was the Hartford Whalers' appointed on-ice leader in 1981-82. Rob Ramage, the Leafs captain from 1989 to 1991, was the last captain of the Colorado Rockies in 1981-82.

17. The Montreal Maroons, under manager Tommy Gorman, hired the King at the start of the 1937-38 season. Clancy's stay was brief, however, and he resigned after only 18 games. The Maroons finished in last place and dropped out of the league at the end of the season.

18. Imlach moved from assistant general manager to general manager to coach in a matter of weeks. When he was named general manager, his first act was to fire coach Billy Reay and appoint himself in Reay's place. Reay went on to coach the Chicago Black Hawks for 14 years.

19. Sid Smith, captain of the Leafs in 1955-56, won the Lady Byng in 1952 and 1955. Dave Keon, captain from 1969 to 1975, captured the Lady Byng Trophy in 1962 and 1963.

20. In 1971-72, Clancy took over the Leafs after coach John McLellan suffered a stroke late in the season. Clancy led the Leafs into the playoffs with a record of 9-3-3 in 15 games. The Leafs lost in the opening round of the playoff to the eventual Stanley Cup-champion Boston Bruins. At the end of the season, Clancy was awarded the J.P. Bickell Cup as the Leafs "most valuable player."

21. Alex Romeril was Smythe's right hand man in the early operating days of the franchise, replacing Mike Rodden, who had guided the St. Pats.

22. Charlie Conacher was the first Leafs captain to score 200 goals in his career, reaching that milestone in his only season as Leafs captain in 1937-38. Interestingly, Conacher never scored another goal as a member of the Leafs, finishing his career with Detroit and the New York Americans.

23. Hamilton Tigers goalie Howard Lockhart was Clancy's first victim in Ottawa's 3-2 win over the Tigers on December 17, 1921. Clancy's goal, the overtime winner, came on his first NHL shift.

24. Tom Watt led the Winnipeg Jets to a 33-33-14 record

in 1981-82 to capture the coach of the year honours.

25. The Leafs were without a captain during those years, using a variety of assistants from the day Rick Vaive was removed as captain in 1986 to the start of the 1989-90 season.

26. Rare Jewel was the winning pony in the Coronation Futility and all the numbers were in her favour. She was wearing number 7 and was number 11 on the pole.

27. Frank Selke, Sr., who later went on to manage the Montreal Canadiens to six Stanley Cup titles, began his career as Conn Smythe's assistant in September 1929.

28. Syl Apps was the first Leafs captain to don a "C," putting the official designation on the breast of his uniform in the 1947-48 season.

29. Jimmy Fowler, a 21-year-old speedster from Toronto, joined the Leafs for the 1936-37 season, becoming a regular after Clancy retired. He led all Leaf rearguards in goals in both 1937 and 1938 before being traded to the New York Americans in 1939.

Coaching Corner

Match the name of a Toronto Maple Leafs coach with the years he served in that capacity. Answers on page 125.

Hap Day	1950-51 to 1952-53
Red Kelly	1984-85 to 1985-86
Howie Meeker	1977-78 to 1978-79
Dan Maloney	1940-41 to 1949-50
Joe Primeau	1956-57
Roger Neilson	1973-74 to 1976-77

6

Let's Make a Deal

THE SECRET TO ANY PROFESSIONAL SPORTS TEAM'S success rests in its ability to constantly acquire new talent with shrewd draft selections and savvy trades. Although every team will make errors in judgement, the most successful franchises are those who are able to trade their past for their future.

In many of the Maple Leafs' Stanley Cup victories over the years, a trade has been responsible for supplying that extra spark needed to push the team over the top. This was certainly true in the Leafs' first Cup triumph in 1932. Goaltender Lorne Chabot, defensive leader King Clancy, and role players Harold Darragh and Baldy Cotton were all acquired through trades by Conn Smythe. Although the Leafs went on to the finals six more times under coach Dick Irvin, they failed to win another Stanley Cup until 1942. By that time, the entire roster of the team that had captured the championship in 1932 had changed, with new talent like Sweeney Schriner, Billy Taylor, and Lorne Carr being obtained from other organizations.

The Leafs went on to win five Stanley Cups in the 1940s, and in each of them, a key trade provided the team with a "missing link." Babe Pratt, who scored the Cup-winning goal in 1945, was obtained from the New York Rangers and he provided the team with excellent defence as well as 41 points during the 1944-45 season

In 1946-47, the Leafs were bolstered by the addition of Harry Watson from Detroit. Even Ted Kennedy, who scored the Cup-winning goal for the Leafs in 1947, was originally acquired from the Montreal Canadiens. One of the greatest trades in Leaf history was finalized early in the 1947-48 season when Toronto landed Max Bentley from Chicago. Although the Leafs sacrificed part of their future by sending five players to the Black Hawks, the Leafs won three Stanley Cups in the next four years with Bentley aboard

In the late 1950s, the Leafs completed a decade-long rebuilding process by acquiring Red Kelly from the Detroit Red Wings. Although Kelly's skills as a defenceman were deteriorating, his legs and eyes were still strong. Coach Imlach moved him to centre, where he combined with Frank Mahovlich to give the Leafs a formidable one-two punch. The combination led the Leafs to four Stanley Cups in seven years, and the Kelly trade stands out as Imlach's finest manoeuvre. On the other side of the ledger, Imlach's deal to bring Andy Bathgate from the Rangers paid instant dividends with a Cup victory in 1964, but the five young players Imlach traded went on to play an average of 11 seasons each in the NHL, while Bathgate played only 70 games with the team. However, three of the players Imlach received when he dealt Bathgate to Detroit (Pronovost, Jeffrey, and Erickson) played key roles in the Leafs' last championship in 1967

Many of the Leafs' stars in the last quarter century, such as Paul Henderson, Norm Ullman, Bill Derlago, Rick Vaive, Dan Daoust, and Ed Olczyk, were obtained through trades. Yet, despite the constant roster shuffling, the Leafs were never able to return to their past form. However, in the past two seasons, the Leafs have actively returned to the trading table, and the results have been dramatic. Glenn Anderson, Grant Fuhr, Doug Gilmour, Jamie Macoun, John Cullen, and Dave Andreychuk, were all added by current GM Cliff Fletcher in exchange for players who really didn't have a future with the club. Fletcher and his coaching staff are adamant they will build for the present without sacrificing the future.

Questions

1. In one of the most famous Leaf trades, Toronto obtained Max Bentley from the Chicago Black Hawks. Who went to the Windy City and who came to Canada with Bentley?
2. After being manhandled by the Philadelphia Flyers in three consecutive playoff years, the Leafs obtained some much needed toughness in 1978, but they paid a stiff price. Who did they obtain and what did they give up?
3. Punch Imlach's second stay as Leafs general

manager was unimpressive, but he did swing a deal with the Vancouver Canucks that paid dividends for years. Who were the principals involved?

4. Who was the first player acquired by Cliff Fletcher when he assumed the GM duties in July 1991?

5. The NHL's all-time ironman was a member of the Leafs family briefly, but he was quickly traded before he could play a game for the squad. Name him and the player the Leafs received for him.

6. In 1965, the Leafs made a trade with Springfield of the AHL for a goaltender who would eventually play six seasons with the team. Who was the goalie they received and who did they trade away?

7. In 1946, Smythe attempted – without success – to purchase a player that he had scouted and dismissed years earlier as being "too skinny." Who was the future Hall of Famer whom Smythe missed out on?

8. In 1939, the Leafs sent four players to the New York Americans to obtain that team's lone star. Who was the "star" and what well-known names did the Leafs send to Broadway?

9. In 1943, Frank Selke landed one of the NHL's greatest rearguards from the New York Rangers, despite the fact the Rangers had lost six front-liners to the army. Who was the blueliner who would soon electrify fans at the Gardens?

10. In 1955, the Leafs traded one of the NHL's hardest-hitting defencemen to the Bruins for a player who had been with the Leafs when they won four Cups in five years from 1947-51. Name the two principals in the deal.

11. In 1964, the Leafs completed another trade of

massive proportions, sending five players to the Rangers for the man they hoped would lead the leafs to the Stanley Cup. Name the main player the Leafs received, and the players the Leafs sent to the Rangers, if you can.

12. In the 1969 amateur draft, many Leaf scouts recommended that general manager Jim Gregory select Bobby Clarke. However, when the Leafs' selection arrived, the Leafs chose another player, even though Clarke was available. Who did the Leafs take instead?

13. In 1962, James Norris, boss of the Chicago Black Hawks, thought he had a deal to purchase a key member of the Leafs for a cool million dollars. Who was the hot ticket that Norris wanted to cash in?

14. When the Leafs traded Darryl Sittler to Philadelphia on January 20, 1982, they received a player, a draft choice, and a future consideration. Name the three players they eventually received.

15. In the largest trade in NHL history, the Leafs and Flames exchanged 10 players in January 1992. Can you remember their names?

16. In 1974, the Leafs made a trade involving two players, both of whom went to have 50-goal seasons, but not with the Leafs. Name the two snipers and the teams they fired the 50 goals with.

17. In September 1991, the Leafs acquired a player who had been to the Stanley Cup finals with three different teams in the 1980s. However, he stayed in Toronto for only two games before leaving to play in Italy. Who was he?

18. This future Minnesota North Stars captain, New

York Islanders star, and Team Canada's '72 member was acquired by Toronto on October 3, 1967 along with Bryan Hextall. Who was he?

19. This three-time Second Team All-Star was traded to Toronto by Boston for Ron Stewart in 1965. Can you name him?

20. What three veterans did the Leafs receive for Scott Pearson in 1990?

21. The Leafs have traded their first-round draft selection five times since 1969. They have acquired four players for those five picks; two goalies, a defenceman, and a forward. Can you recall their names and the years the Leafs surrendered their selections?

22. This 1982 Leaf draft choice scored 39 goals for the Bruins in 1991-92. Who is he and what team did the Leafs originally trade him to?

23. An era in Maple Leaf Gardens came to an end in 1968 when the Leafs traded Frank Mahovlich to the Detroit Red Wings. Who were the other players involved?

24. In June 1967, the Leafs traded Red Kelly to the Los Angeles Kings so Kelly could become the Kings' first coach. Whom did the Leafs receive in return?

25. In 1970, Toronto, St. Louis, and the New York Rangers had a three-way trade arranged that would have seen three future Hall of Famers change teams. Although the first portion of the deal was completed in March, it was never closed. Can you name the three Famers involved and outline the strange circumstance that prevented it from occurring?

26. In 1978, the Leafs unloaded a future Norris Trophy

winner and a forward for a hard-nosed defenceman. Name the three players involved.

27. This Hall of Fame defenceman, who was virtually "booed off Broadway" when he was with the Rangers, was obtained from the Boston Bruins for another defenceman who had started his career as a Bruin. Name both parties.

28. This future NHL coach was traded by the Leafs to the New York Rangers in 1964, before he ever had the opportunity to play in Toronto. Can you name him?

29. This all-time great, who played on four Stanley Cup winners with Ottawa, finished his career in Toronto. Can you name him and the player Conn Smythe sent to the Senators to obtain him?

30. In one of Conn Smythe's wisest purchases, this right-winger was bought from the New York Americans in 1942. He went on to lead the team in goals twice. Who was he?

31. In 1953, Conn Smythe sold one of the league's classiest players to the New York Rangers so he could finish his career with his brother. Who was he?

32. In 1962, the Leafs sent five players (four defencemen and one forward) to the Springfield Indians for a temperamental AHL rearguard. One of the defencemen involved went on to star with Team Canada '72. Can you name the player the Leafs received and the future Team Canada star?

33. One of the Buffalo Sabres' finest defensive forwards in the 1970s, this player finished his career with the Leafs in 1981-82. Who is he?

34. This player, a first-round draft selection of the

Kansas City Scouts in 1976, was traded to the Leafs from Colorado in 1979, but he was quickly dispatched to Pittsburgh, where he scored 34 goals in his first season. Who was he?

Answers

1. The Leafs sent the entire "Flying Forts" trio of Bodnar, Poile, and Stewart, as well as Ernie Dickens and Bob Goldham, to Chicago for Bentley and Cy Thomas, who played only eight games for the Leafs.
2. Toronto received Dan Maloney from Detroit for Errol Thompson and the Leafs' first-round draft selections in the 1978 and 1980 Entry Drafts.
3. Toronto sent Tiger Williams and Jerry "Bugsy" Butler to the Canucks for Bill Derlago and Rick Vaive.
4. Anxious to obtain some scoring touch up front, Fletcher sent a third-round draft choice in the 1993 Entry Draft to the Philadelphia Flyers for Mike Bullard. Unfortunately, Bullard had lost most of his skills, scoring only 14 goals for the team.
5. Doug Jarvis was selected by the Leafs 24th overall in the 1975 draft and quickly dealt to the Canadiens for Greg Hubiuk. Jarvis played 964 consecutive games in the NHL, Hubiuk played 25 games for the Leafs.
6. The Leafs sent Larry Johnston (who played to 320 games in the NHL) and Bill Smith to Springfield for Bruce Gamble, who recorded 16 shutouts in his tenure with Toronto from 1965-66 to February 1, 1971.
7. Milt Schmidt, who attended a Leafs training session

in the mid-1930s, became one of Boston's most famous Bruins.

8. Toronto obtained Dave "Sweeney" Schriner, a two-time Art Ross Trophy winner, for Busher Jackson, Buzz Boll, Murray Armstrong, and Doc Romnes. Sweeney was the spark the Leafs needed, and they won a pair of Cup titles with him in the lineup.

9. Babe Pratt, whose freewheeling ways on and off the ice made him expendable in New York, came to the Leafs for Hank Goldup and a young rookie named Red Garrett. Garrett would soon become the first NHL player to lose his life during the Second World War.

10. Toronto sent future Hall of Famer Leo Boivin to Boston for ex-Leaf Joe Klukay. Klukay played only 74 more games before retiring while Boivin played another 1,000 games in the NHL.

11. Andy Bathgate, the Rangers' all-time leading scorer, did help the Leafs win the Cup in 1964, but he was dispatched to Detroit after only 70 games in a Leaf uniform. The players the Leafs sent to the Rangers – Bob Nevin, Rod Seiling, Dick Duff, Arnie Brown, and Bill Collins – played a total of 61 more seasons in the league.

12. The Leafs chose Ernie Mosher from Estevan. Worried about Clarke's diabetes, the Leafs shied away from him, even though Harold Ballard himself was a diabetic and knew Clarke could survive the rigours of pro hockey. Mosher never played in the NHL.

13. At an All-Star Game party, Norris and Harold Ballard struck a deal to send Frank Mahovlich to the

Hawks for seven figures in cash. Norris even wrote a cheque for the amount, but the deal didn't have the approval of the board of directors and never was consummated.

14. The Leafs received Rich Costello (10 games) and Ken Strong (15 games) from the Flyers for their all-time leading scorer. With the draft selection, Toronto chose Peter Ihnacak (417 games).

15. Toronto sent Jeff Reese, Gary Leeman, Alex Godynyuk, Craig Berube, and Michel Petit to Calgary for Doug Gilmour, Ric Natress, Jamie Macoun, Rick Wamsley, and Kent Manderville on January 2, 1992.

16. The Leafs sent Rick Kehoe (55 goals in 1980-81) to Pittsburgh for Blaine Stoughton (56 goals in 1980 and 52 goals in 1982 with Hartford). Stoughton jumped from the Leafs to the WHA after only 121 games, and was later claimed by Hartford in the expansion draft.

17. Ken Linseman played in the finals with Philadelphia, Edmonton, and Boston in the 1980s.

18. J.P. Parise, who had 20-goal seasons for the Islanders, North Stars, and the Cleveland Barons, was obtained by the Leafs in exchange for Gerry Ehman.

19. Pat Stapleton, a fixture on the Black Hawks defence for eight seasons, was claimed by Chicago on the waiver wire less than 24 hours after being acquired by Toronto in June 1965.

20. Michel Petit, Aaron Broten, and Claude Loiselle were obtained from the Quebec Nordiques on November 17, 1990.

21. Toronto received Bernie Parent for their #1 pick in 1971, Wayne Thomas for their #1 pick in 1976, Dan

Maloney for their #1 picks in 1978 and 1980, and Tom Kurvers for the #1 selection in the 1991 draft.

22. Vladimir Ruzicka was the Leafs' fifth selection in the 1982 Entry Draft. Toronto dealt him to Edmonton for a fourth-round draft pick (Greg Walters) in 1989.

23. Norm Ullman, Floyd Smith, and Paul Henderson came to Toronto in exchange for the Big M, Garry Unger, Pete Stemkowski, and the rights to Carl Brewer.

24. The Leafs received defenceman Ken Block for Red Kelly's rights. Block never played for the Leafs. Instead, he played seven seasons in the WHA.

25. On March 3, 1970, after 20 years in a Leafs uniform, Tim Horton was traded to the New York Rangers for future considerations. Those considerations involved a three-way deal to send Jacques Plante to Toronto and Terry Sawchuk to the St. Louis Blues from the New York Rangers. However, just before the deal was to be finalized, Sawchuk died. The Leafs received Guy Trottier and Denis Dupere for Horton and purchased Plante from the St. Louis Blues.

26. Toronto sent Randy Carlyle and George Ferguson to the Pittsburgh Penguins for Dave Burrows. Burrows played just 86 games for Toronto before being sent back to Pittsburgh while Carlyle continued to play in the NHL until 1992-93. Ferguson had four consecutive 20-goal seasons for the Penguins.

27. The Leafs received Allan Stanley from the Bruins for Jim Morrison, who had started his career with Boston. Stanley became an All-Star defenceman with the Leafs, while Morrison was bounced from the Bruins

to the Red Wings to the Rangers. Morrison then played eight seasons with the AHL's Quebec Aces before making it back to the show with Pittsburgh in 1970.

28. Lou Angotti, who went on to coach the St. Louis Blues, was signed by the Leafs from Michigan Tech University and assigned to the AHL's Rochester Americans. He was traded to the New York Rangers for defenceman Duane Rupp.

29. Frank Nighbor, the "Pembroke Peach," came to the Leafs in exchange for Dan Cox.

30. Lorne Carr was bought by Smythe after the 1940-41 season. He scored 36 goals and established a team record with 74 points in 1943-44.

31. Max Bentley went to the Rangers, where he finished his career with his brother Doug.

32. The Leafs sent Wally Boyer, Dick Mattiussi, Rollie Wilcox, Bill White, and Roger Cote to Springfield for Kent Douglas, who won the Calder Trophy in 1963. White was traded by the Los Angeles Kings (who purchased the Springfield team in 1967) to Chicago, where he starred for seven seasons.

33. Don Luce, who compiled six consecutive seasons with at least 20 goals, came to the Leafs from the Los Angeles Kings for Bob Gladney.

34. Paul Gardner, who became an AHL scoring champion in his later years, was acquired by Toronto for Don Ashby and Trevor Johansen. The players the Leafs received for Gardner when they sent him to Pittsburgh – Paul Marshall and Kim Davis – played a total of 25 games for the Leafs.

Do You Know Me?

The following players began the 1991-92 season with Toronto but were traded to another team or were picked up on waivers by another team during the season. Can you name the players and the team each finished the season with? Answers on pages 125-6.

1

2

3

4

5

6

The Cup and the Champions

ON APRIL 9, 1932, IN FRONT OF A PACKED HOUSE IN
Maple Leaf Gardens, the Toronto Maple Leafs defeated
the New York Rangers 6-4 to win the first Stanley Cup in
the franchise's young history. It was a moment of sweet
revenge for manager Conn Smythe, who had been fired
as manager of the New York Rangers in 1926 before the
team even took to the ice. The team that Smythe built in
New York went on to win the Stanley Cup in its second
season, but Smythe received none of the credit. However,
in 1932, he took a full bow as the Leafs, only five seasons
old, skated into the winner's circle for the first time.

Over the next ten years the Leafs would make six
more unsuccessful trips to the finals before winning
another championship in 1942. In that final against the
Detroit Red Wings, the Leafs dropped the opening three
games before storming back to win the next four to
become the only team in the history of professional sport

to win a best-of-seven championship round after losing the first three contests.

In 1945, the Leafs regained their championship status, thanks to a herculean effort by goaltender Frank McCool. McCool, a 26-year-old amateur brought in to replace Turk Broda, who was in the army, won the Calder Trophy as best rookie and recorded four shutouts in the playoffs to lead the Leafs to victory. McCool suffered from inoperable ulcers, an ailment that would eventually take his life. Midway through game seven of the final, he skated off the ice clutching his stomach, unable to stand the pressure and the pain. Leaf coach Hap Day followed him to the dressing room, sat down beside him and simply said, "There's no one else, Frank." McCool looked up, took a slug of milk to settle his nerves and returned to the nets, where he shut down the Wings and guided the Leafs to a decisive 2-1 victory.

There are numerous other heroes, such as Don Simmons, who came in to replace an injured Johnny Bower in game four of the 1962 finals, and won games five and six in the last playoff appearances of his career. Terry Sawchuk's efforts in the 1967 playoffs rivalled any performance of his esteemed career.

But there are two other men who truly qualify as Stanley Cup heroes. In the 1951 finals against Montreal, every match went into overtime. In game five, defenceman Bill Barilko spotted a loose puck and dove in from the blueline to backhand the disc over goalie Gerry McNeil to win the Cup for Toronto. It was the last goal of his career as he was killed in a plane crash during the summer of 1951. Barilko's number "5" has never been worn by a Leaf since the 1951 finals.

Perhaps the greatest Leaf hero is Bobby Baun, who scored the winning goal in game six of the 1964 finals against Detroit while playing with a broken ankle. In the third period of a tied game, with the Wings needing a single victory to win their first Stanley Cup since 1955, Baun stopped a shot on his ankle and was forced to visit the dressing room. He insisted the trainer wrap the limb tight, and he returned to the bench for overtime, eventually winning the game when his shot from the point eluded Terry Sawchuk in the Wings' net. Baun played the next game as well, a 4-0 Cup-clinching win for Toronto, before allowing the X-rays that confirmed what he already knew: the ankle was fractured.

There will be other heroes in other times, Doug Gilmour or Felix Potvin, perhaps. But for the time being, these men hold a special place on the Maple Leafs' Stanley Cup honour roll.

Questions

1. When the Leafs defeated the New York Rangers to win their first Stanley Cup in 1932, it was called the "tennis series." Why?
2. In the 1933 semi-finals, the Leafs needed an overtime goal to defeat the Montreal Maroons and advance to their first Cup final. Who scored the series-clinching winner?
3. When Toronto made its miracle comeback in the 1942 finals, they were aided by an odd incident at the conclusion of game four. What was the episode?
4. In the 1943 semi-finals, Detroit avenged their 1942

loss by defeating the Leafs in six games. The Wings won game six on an overtime goal by a player who had spent the entire season in the minors. Can you name him?

5. In the 1933 finals, the Rangers defeated the Leafs in four games, capturing the series on the only Stanley Cup-winning goal to be scored on a powerplay in overtime. In fact, the Leafs had two men in the penalty box. Can you name the famous Ranger who scored the goal and the two Leafs who watched it from the sin-bin?

6. In the 1945 finals, the Leafs established a Stanley Cup record by shutting out the Red Wings for 128 consecutive minutes. Who was the goaltender who achieved the feat and what was his famous nickname?

7. In the 1993 playoffs, the Leafs set a team record for fewest shots allowed in a playoff period. Who were the Leafs' opponents and how many shots did they register?

8. On March 23, 1944, Maurice Richard scored all five goals in a 5-1 victory over the Leafs in game two of the semi-finals. Who was the goaltender who was victimized by the Rocket's red glare?

9. In game two of the 1949 finals, the Leafs scored two powerplay goals on the same penalty. In fact, the same man scored both goals. Can you name him?

10. On April 14, 1959, the Leafs won their first game in the Stanley Cup finals since Bill Barilko scored the Cup winner in 1951, needing overtime to secure a 3-2 win over Montreal. Who scored the goal that put the Leafs back in the series?

11. In game four of the 1959 finals, Montreal exploded for three goals in six minutes to win the game 3-2. Name the Montreal player who scored the game winner and assisted on the other two.

12. Who scored the first ever playoff goal for the Toronto Maple Leafs?

13. In the 1938 finals, the Leafs met the Chicago Black Hawks, who were forced to employ a substitute goaltender in game one because Mike Karakas, their regular netminder, was injured. Who was the substitute goalie who stoned the Leafs in the series opener?

14. In game three of the 1979 quarterfinals, the Leafs lost in double overtime to the Montreal Canadiens, giving the Habs a 3-0 lead in games. Who scored the heartbreaking goal for Montreal?

15. Toronto's mid-1970s playoff confrontations with Philadelphia were legendary. In 1977, the Leafs won the first two games of the series at the Spectrum before losing game three in overtime. In game four, the Leafs had a 5-2 advantage with five minutes remaining, but the Flyers stormed back to win 6-5 in overtime. Who scored the overtime winner?

16. Can you name the Leaf forward who led all post-season scorers in the 1936 playoffs?

17. This right-winger is the last forward to win back-to-back Stanley Cups with different teams, winning the Cup with the Leafs in 1962. Name him.

18. In the first game of the 1963 finals, this Toronto forward set an NHL record for the fastest two goals from the start of a Stanley Cup final game. Name the quick-triggered Maple Leaf and the time it took for him to fire his pair of goals.

19. Lanny McDonald set a team record during the 1977 playoffs. What mark did McDonald establish?

20. Darryl Sittler added his name to the record books with a record performance against Philadelphia in the 1976 quarterfinals. What was his record and what else was unique about it?

21. The first NHL player to fire a hat-trick in a single play-off period was a Maple Leaf. Who was he and what team did he victimize?

22. This former Leaf coach is the only man to coach three different teams in the Stanley Cup finals. Who is he?

23. These two former Leaf goaltenders were the first rookies ever to face each other in a Stanley Cup final game. Name the two freshmen, the two teams, and the year this famous event occurred.

24. In the 1959 semi-finals, the Leafs dropped the first two games to Boston, but stormed back to win games three and four in overtime. Two different players were sudden-death marksmen for the Leafs. Name them.

25. Before Mike Foligno's overtime goal on Tim Cheveldae in game five of the 1993 divisional semi-finals, who was the last Leaf to score an overtime winner and who was the victim.

26. This former Toronto Maple Leaf first-round draft selection played only two playoff games for the Leafs, but scored a goal in each of them. Can you name him?

27. The Leafs' attempt to win four straight Cups during the 1960s was halted by the Montreal Canadiens, who eliminated Toronto 4 games to 2 in 1965. The Habs won the decisive sixth game in overtime on a

goal by the only man to help win at least eight Stanley Cups and not be in the Hall of Fame. Who was he?

28. In 1962, the Leafs met the New York Rangers in the playoffs for the first time in 20 years. In an evenly played series, Toronto needed an overtime goal in game five to take a 3-2 lead in games. Who scored the winner for the Leafs and who was the victim?

29. Dave Andreychuk set a playoff record for the Leafs during the 1993 playoffs. What record did he set and whose record did he break?

30. In his first ever post-season appearance, Felix Potvin became the seventh Leaf goaltender to play over 20 career playoff games. Name the other six goalies.

31. Besides "Busher" Jackson, two other Maple Leaf players have scored hat-tricks in a single period during the playoffs. Can you name them?

32. The Leafs hold the NHL record for fewest goals allowed in a series that went six games. Who were the Leafs' opponents and how many goals did they allow?

33. Who led the Maple Leafs in playoff scoring in 1959, the first season they reached the finals since 1951?

34. In the 1978 playoffs, the Leafs set an NHL record with three goals in 23 seconds. Can you name the two players who accounted for the three goals and the team they played against?

35. In one of the Maple Leafs' darker playoff moments, the Boston Bruins trampled the Leafs 10-0 in game one of the 1969 playoffs. One former Leaf player set a record for penalties and the Bruins set a record for powerplay goals. Who was the penalized player and

how many goals did the Bruins score with the Leafs a man short?

36. Before Felix Potvin whitewashed the St. Louis Blues in game seven of the Norris finals, who was the last Leaf rookie goaltender to record a playoff shutout and what team did he blank?

37. This former Leaf coach has the best winning percentage in the history of the Stanley Cup finals. Who is he?

38. Name the only Leaf goalie to face a penalty shot in the playoffs. Who took the shot and what was the result?

39. Hap Day won ten playoff series and lost only four in his career as a coach. What teams did he lose those four series to?

Answers

1. It was called the "tennis series" because the Leafs won the three games by scores of 6-4, 6-2, 6-4

2. Bob Gracie, who played on a line with Frank Finnigan and Andy Blair, scored at 17:59 of the first overtime to eliminate the Maroons and send the Leafs to their first Stanley Cup final.

3. In the closing minutes of game four, with the Leafs leading by one goal, referee Mel Harwood gave a misconduct penalty to Detroit's Eddie Wares. On the ensuing faceoff, he also whistled the Wings for having too many men on the ice. This penalty was served by Don Grosso who, at one point, left the penalty box

and dropped his gloves at Harwood's feet. After the game, Detroit coach and manager Jack Adams pursued Harwood across the ice and punched him before being restrained by the linesmen. Adams was suspended for the rest of the series and Wares and Grosso were fined. As for Harwood, he never refereed in the NHL again.

4. The goal was scored by Adam Brown, a renowned soccer player in the off-season, who spent the entire season with the Indianapolis Caps, the Wings farm squad.

5. Bill Cook scored the winner at 7:33 of overtime with Alex Levinsky and Bill Thoms' in the penalty box. It was Thoms only penalty of the series and one of only three he received in 44 playoff games during his career.

6. Frank "Ulcers" McCool was the shutout king in the only playoff appearances of his career. His constant stomach problems limited him to only 72 NHL games.

7. The Leafs held the Los Angeles Kings to only one shot in the third period of game one in the 1993 Campbell Conference finals.

8. Paul Bibeault, who led the league with five shutouts during the season, allowed all five goals by Richard, who was named as the game's first, second, and third star by Foster Hewitt.

9. Sid Smith scored a pair of goals with Pete Horeck in the penalty box, then set an NHL record with a third powerplay goal in the second period, providing all the offense in the Leafs' 3-1 victory. It wasn't until

the 1956-57 season that the NHL introduced the rule that enabled a player to leave the penalty box if his team was scored upon.

10. Dick Duff scored at the 10:06 mark of overtime to give the Leafs their only win of the series.

11. Bernie "Boom-Boom" Geoffrion single-handedly put Montreal one game away from the Stanley Cup title with assists on Ab McDonald's and Ralph Backstrom's goals before scoring the winner himself.

12. Andy Blair scored Toronto's first playoff goal in the Leafs' 3-1 victory over Detroit in game one of the 1929 quarter-finals.

13. Alfie Moore, who had never appeared in a playoff game before, allowed a goal on the first shot he faced but stopped all the rest as Chicago won the game 3-1. It was the only playoff victory in Moore's brief career.

14. Cam Connor, a first-round draft selection of the Canadiens, scored a breakaway goal on Mike Palmateer to give the Habs the victory. It was the only playoff goal Connor would score in his career for Montreal.

15. Reggie Leach scored the overtime winner at the 19:10 mark of the first overtime. The Flyers, who had three players – Moose Dupont, Gary Dornhoefer, and Ross Lonsberry – ejected from the game, scored three goals in the final five minutes of regulation to tie the game.

16. Buzz Boll compiled seven goals and ten points in the 1936 playoffs, the only playoff points of his entire career.

17. Ed Litzenberger, the last player to be traded midway

through the year he won the Calder Trophy as rookie of the year, won the Cup with Chicago in 1961 and Toronto in 1962.

18. Dick Duff scored two goals in 68 seconds, both on assists from Allan Stanley, to give the Leafs a quick lead they never relinquished.

19. Lanny, who fired three goals against Pittsburgh and four goals against Philadelphia, became the first Maple Leaf to record two hat-tricks in the same play-off year.

20. Sittler became only the third player in NHL history to score five goals in a single playoff game in Toronto's 8-5 victory in game six of the quarter-finals. They were the only goals Sittler scored in the entire post-season.

21. "Busher" Jackson scored three goals in the second period of game one of the 1932 Stanley Cup finals against the New York Rangers.

22. Dick Irvin led the Black Hawks (1931), Maple Leafs (seven times), and the Montreal Canadiens (eight times) to the Stanley Cup finals.

23. On April 6, 1945, Detroit's Harry Lumley (who later played for the Leafs in the mid-1950s) and the Leafs' Frank McCool became the first rookie goaltenders to face each other in a Stanley Cup final game.

24. Gerry Ehman scored at 5:02 of extra time in game three and Frank Mahovlich scored at 11:21 of overtime in game four. Ehman had a hand in that victory as well. Bruins winger Jean-Guy Gendron was in the penalty box serving a major for crosschecking Ehman when the Big M potted the winner. It was the first playoff goal of Mahovlich's career.

25. In game five of the Norris Division semi-finals, Ed Olczyk scored at 0:34 seconds against Greg Stefan and the Detroit Red Wings.

26. Scott Pearson scored two goals in the 1990 Norris Division semi-finals against the St. Louis Blues, his only playoff appearances with the Leafs before being dealt to Quebec.

27. Claude Provost slipped the puck past Johnny Bower after 16:33 of overtime in game six. Provost played on eight Cup winners in Montreal from 1955 to 1969, but has yet to find his way into the Hall of Fame.

28. Red Kelly scored on the Rangers' Gump Worsley after 24 minutes of overtime to put the Leafs one game away from their third finals appearance in four years. In game six, they scored six goals in the first period on their way to a 7-1 victory.

29. Andreychuk scored 12 playoff goals in the 1993 play-offs, eclipsing Lanny McDonald's record 10 goals during the 1977 post-season.

30. The six goalies are Turk Broda (102gp), Johnny Bower (74gp), Mike Palmateer (29gp), Ken Wregget (25gp), Lorne Chabot (22gp), and George Hainsworth (21gp).

31. Darryl Sittler (April 22, 1976 vs. Philadelphia) and George Ferguson (April 11, 1978 vs. Los Angeles). Ferguson's hat-trick, in the Leafs' first game of the 1978 playoffs, matched his career total in 29 post-season games.

32. An odd set of circumstances created this record, for although the record is for a six-game series, the Leafs won the set in five games. The Leafs allowed only five goals in their 1951 semi-final against the Boston

Bruins, winning the series four games to one, with one game ending in a 1-1 tie. A curfew rule in Toronto prevented game two from being played past the first overtime period. As in the 1988 finals, when a power failure ended a Boston-Edmonton game in a 3-3 tie, the statistics still count.

33. Gerry Ehman had the playoff of a lifetime with six goals and seven assists for 13 points in 1959. Ehman played 18 more playoff games for the Leafs during his career and compiled one assist.

34. Darryl Sittler scored a pair of goals at 4:04 and 4:16 and Ron Ellis added a single marker at 4:27 on April 12, 1979, against the Atlanta Flames.

35. Forbes Kennedy compiled 38 penalty minutes in the game, including a game misconduct and suspension for slugging linesman George Ashley. The Bruins scored a record six powerplay goals during the game.

36. Although Ken Wregget had played games during the 1983-84 and 1984-85 seasons, he was still considered a rookie during the 1985-86 season. He shut out the St. Louis Blues 3-0 on April 20, 1986.

37. Hap Day compiled a 20-8 mark in the Stanley Cup finals, for a record winning percentage of .714.

38. Petr Klima scored on Allan Bester in Detroit's 6-3 win over Toronto in game three of the 1988 Norris Division semi-finals.

39. Day lost to Boston (seven games in 1941), Detroit (six games in 1943), Montreal (five games in 1944), and Detroit (seven games in 1950).

Cup Pucksters

During the 1960s the Toronto Maple Leafs won four Stanley Cup championships. Below are the seasons the team won the Cup during that decade. Under each season four players are listed, two of whom were either traded during the year or played 10 games or less during the regular schedule and thus were ineligible to have their names engraved on the Stanley Cup. Circle the two players whose names appear on the Stanley Cup for the specific season indicated. Answers on page 126.

1961-62
Eddie Shack, Bob Pulford, Arnie Brown, Larry Keenan

1962-63
Kent Douglas, Rod Seiling, Al Arbour, Ron Stewart

1963-64
Dick Duff, Jim Pappin, Gerry Ehman, Ron Ellis

1966-67
Wayne Carleton, Brit Selby, Marcel Pronovost, Milan Marcetta

ACROSS

1. Pictured player.
5. Son of Cal played with Leafs. (initials)
7. Goaltender with Leafs in late '60s. (initials)
9. Led Leafs in scoring in '92-93.
12. All hockey arenas have this in case of fire.
13. A player's instincts.
15. Played with Sittler and McDonald. (initials)
16. After time in the minors, one has _____ his dues.
19. Goaltender on Leafs 1932 team. (initials)
20. Last coach to guide Leafs to Cup win.
22. The Cat.
24. Brother of Peter and Anton. (initials)
25. Had team record eleven 20-goal seasons.
26. Former Leafs coach and G.M. has trophy named after him.
28. Fan favourite, traded to Colorado.
29. An Ottawa-born King.
30. Tiger. (initials)
31. Bill Barilko wore this number.
32. Leafs goaltender traded to Flames. (initials)
33. Bob Baun broke this.
35. In play at all times.
38. Defenceman began NHL career with Leafs in '49-50.
39. Young Leafs defenceman later played sevens seasons in WHA.
41. Defensive centreman with the Leafs in the '80s.
42. Players sometimes go here after a game.
43. Led Leafs in scoring in '86-87.
46. Offensive defenceman often uses this tactic.
47. Ends only when goal is scored. (initials)
48. Won three Cups each with Leafs and Canadiens. (initials)
49. Led Leafs in scoring in '63-64, '66-67, and '69-70.
51. Jr. also played in NHL.
55. Goaltender traded to Oilers.
57. Holds record for defenceman with five goals in one game.
58. Holds Leafs team record for career shutouts.
59. Became captain of Leafs prior to '48-49 season. (initials)
60. Leafs were in this division before moving to Adams.
63. Hockey is played on this.
66. Former Leafs player coached team in the '80s.
67. First team captain of Leafs. (initials)
68. Acquired by Leafs during '92-93 season.

DOWN

1. Leafs won this three consecutive seasons.
2. Shares name with famous rock singer.
3. Two points for this.
4. Hired as assistant coach in 1989.
5. Czech national played eight seasons with Leafs. (initials)
6. Second Leaf to score 50 goals in a season. (initials)
7. Former Canadiens player won one Cup with Leafs. (initials)
8. Star with Blues started NHL career with Leafs. (initials)
10. Home ice.
11. He and Mr. Spock share first name.
14. Goaltender began NHL career with Leafs in '72-73.
17. Leaf defenceman traded to Capitals. (initials)
18. Andy Bathgate wore this number for Leafs. (Roman numeral)
21. Peanuts character created by hockey fan Charles M. Schulz.
23. Shares part of name with Canadiens star and Islanders star.
27. Came to Leafs after trade with Red Wings.
31. Goaltender traded to Leafs in '73.
32. Defenceman compared to Bobby Orr during junior career.
34. The Entertainer. (initials)
36. Chosen first overall by Leafs in entry draft.
37. Scored one goal for Leafs in '92-93 season.
40. First Leaf to score 40 goals in a season.
41. Died in car accident at age 26. (initials)
42. As Habs are to Canadiens, _____ are to

Maple Leafs.

43. To slow the progress of an opposing player.

44. First Leaf to score 50 goals in a season. (initials)

45. Forerunner of NHL. (initials)

50. Dave Hannan wore this number.

52. Only Leafs coach to win Adams Trophy.

53. Selected third overall by Leafs in '89 Entry Draft. (initials)

54. Leafs defenceman drafted by Canucks in '70 Expansion Draft.

56. Won Calder Trophy (Rookie of the Year) in '43-44.

61. Long-time Sabre spent final NHL season with Leafs. (initials)

62. French abbreviation of NHL.

64. Goaltender

played every game for Leafs in '56-57 and '57-58.

65. Defenceman on Leafs '67 Cup-winning team.

66. Traded to Leafs for John McIntyre. (initials)

Solution on p. 126.

8

Who Am I?

Most passionate hockey fans will remember the great Leaf players of the past, and many will certainly recall the 42 members of the Hockey Hall of Fame who have worn the Maple Leafs jersey throughout the years. However, there have been a number of players whose names deserve a special place in team history if only because many of them made their marks with other organizations

The NHL's first rookie of the year, Carl Voss, started his career in Toronto – in fact, he was the first player ever signed to the team, inked to a contract by Conn Smythe on February 15, 1927, the day after the St. Pats officially became the Maple Leafs. Other notable names of the early years who have gone unnoticed by most Maple Leaf enthusiasts include Hec Kilrea, one of five Ottawa-born Kilreas to play in the NHL. Hec played only two seasons with the Leafs, but he was a main factor in Ottawa's and Detroit's Stanley Cup victories in 1927 and 1936, respectively. Another Leaf whose name has escaped with the sands of time is George Parsons, who lost an eye after a high stick clipped him in 1939. After that incident, the NHL ruled that all players must have complete sight in both eyes, an edict that kept players like Baz Bastien and Greg Neeld out of the league in later years

In the 1940s, three men who never played for the team became heroes for sacrificing their lives during the Second World War. Jack Fox, Red Tilson, and Dudley "Red" Garrett were all members of the Leafs' farm system, and their memories were immortalized on Maple Leaf calendars of the day.

After capturing four Stanley Cups in five years from 1947 to 1951, the Maple Leafs struggled until Punch Imlach came aboard in 1958. However, they did have a number of fine prospects who were allowed to move on to other organizations. When the Boston Bruins made the Stanley Cup finals in 1958, their roster included Fernie Flaman, Jack Bionda, Fleming MacKell, Leo Boivin, and Harry Lumley, all of whom had come to the Bruins from the Maple Leafs' system

Even more prospects slid through the fingers of the club's system in the 1960s. This was not surprising since the Leafs were a winning franchise in both the NHL and the AHL, and their farm system was constantly being weeded in the waiver draft. It was said that the AHL's Rochester Americans, the richest resource in the Leafs' system, was a better team than half of the NHL franchises in the mid-1960s. This was not an idle boast. The 1966 team included 23 players who played, or would play in the NHL, including Garry Unger, Jim Pappin, Don

McKenney, Dick Gamble, Darryl Edestrand, Bronco Horvath, and Don Cherry. Other players, like Wally Boyer, Tim Ecclestone, Rod Seiling, Gerry Cheevers, Eddie Joyal, J.P. Parise, and Bill Sutherland, each of whom made strong contributions to other teams, played for the Leafs during the decade and were lost to other teams. It was a case of the Leafs simply having too much talent.

In the past quarter century, other notable names, like Stoughton, Kehoe, Carlyle, Parent, Thomas, and Nylund have been allowed to leave, but the Leafs are reversing that trend by carefully rebuilding the farm system, signing their prospects to long-term contracts, and steadfastly maintaining their talent base.

Questions

1. Although I was the first Leaf selected in the 1963 Amateur Draft, I never played with the team until 1978. Who am I?

2. I scored the first goal for the Leafs in their first full season in 1927-28. I later won the Stanley Cup with the Boston Bruins. Who am I?

3. I am a member of the 1992-93 Leafs who played for the Canadian Olympic Team before I joined the NHL in 1980. Who am I?

4. I went undefeated in my first NHL season in 1980-81, winning three games and tying one before becoming a regular the next season. I joined the Leafs in 1992.

5. A first-round draft choice of the Detroit Red Wings after leading the OHA in points, I scored 36 goals in

my rookie year with the Wings before joining the Leafs late in my career.

6. Drafted by the Leafs in 1979, I was the first captain of the expansion Ottawa Senators.

7. I set an NHL record by appearing in 517 NHL games before finally making a playoff appearance. The leading scorer in American college hockey in 1980-81 with 47 goals and 59 assists in 45 games, I played briefly for the Leafs in 1990-91.

8. I was the first Leaf to record 300 minutes in penalties in a single season since Tiger Williams in 1978.

9. I missed the entire 1987-88 season with injuries sustained in a car accident.

10. I scored my first NHL goal in the 1993 playoffs.

11. I played with Rick Vaive on the Birmingham Baby Bulls as a 19-year-old underage junior in 1979 and later spent two full seasons with the Leafs.

12. A noted goal scorer, I led the Leafs in penalty minutes in 1988.

13. I tied for the NHL lead in goals in 1936-37, the only year of my career that I scored more than 20 goals in a single season.

14. I led the Leafs in goals scored for five consecutive years during the early 1950s.

15. After making my NHL debut with the Leafs in 1969-70, I jumped to the WHA where I was one of the first WHA players to score 50 goals in a season.

16. An original member of the 1979-80 Edmonton Oilers, I played three seasons with the Leafs, scoring 42 goals in 150 games.

17. One of the few NHLers to wear a moustache in the

1940s, I retired after only four NHL seasons to return to the family farm.

18. Although I never played for the Leafs, I am part of the organization now. I scored 20 goals for three different teams in my 12-year career.

19. I scored at least 30 goals for the Leafs for four consecutive seasons and continue to star in the minor leagues. I was named as the AHL's MVP in 1991-92.

20. I was traded to Toronto with Billy Harris for Ian Turnbull.

21. In my only year with the Leafs I compiled 50 points, the second-best total among team defencemen. I then went on to star with the Italian National Team.

22. In my first five NHL seasons, I compiled only 32 goals. However, with the Leafs in 1981-82, I scored 23 goals and followed that up with a 25-goal effort the following season.

23. I scored my only NHL goal as a member of the Leafs in 1954-55, but I went on to score 525 goals in the AHL.

24. A member of the Leafs for three seasons in the late 1970s, I was recently named as the first coach of the Mighty Ducks of Anaheim.

25. One of only two 20-goal scorers on the original Philadelphia Flyers team in 1967-68, I joined the Leafs the following season, but was returned to the Flyers after collecting only 12 points in 44 games.

26. I played eight games with the Leafs in 1945-46 and never played again in the NHL until the 1955-56 playoffs, when I replaced Gump Worsley in net for the Rangers.

27. I served as Lorne Chabot's backup for three seasons until 1932, but returned to the Leafs 12 seasons later in 1943-44.

28. A hard-hitting defenceman who played for the Leafs from 1987-1991, I am best remembered for a check I laid on New York Rangers rookie Tony Granato during the 1988-89 season.

29. Noted for my lack of hair and my hard-nosed style, I came to the Leafs from the Pittsburgh Pirates for Gerry Lowrey.

30. I was Conn Smythe's paperboy and I pestered him daily until he gave me a tryout. Once I made the team, I was a permanent fixture for 12 seasons.

31. A member of the original Maple Leaf team, I was traded to the New York Rangers in the Lorne Chabot deal and spent 10 productive seasons in New York.

32. I came to the Leafs in 1965, but I made my NHL mark with the Los Angeles Kings, leading the team in goals in their second season and reaching the 20-goal plateau three times.

33. A noted faceoff specialist, I usually spend my summers playing professional soccer.

34. As a rookie in 1981-82, I led the Detroit Red Wings in scoring, but I'm a defensive specialist with the Maple Leafs now.

35. A former Bruin and Maple Leaf, I was traded for two of the NHL's roughest customers, Chris Nilan and Tie Domi, all on the same day!

36. I broke Frank Mahovlich's team record for points by a left-winger.

37. I was the Maple Leafs' first selection in the 1980 Entry

Draft, but I played only 19 games with the club before becoming a Stanley Cup winner with another team.

38. I was the first centreman to score 40 goals in a season for the Leafs since Darryl Sittler.

39. Although my best year with the Leafs was a 28-goal season in 1982-83, my first year with the New York Rangers, I scored 40 goals. Who am I?

Answers

1. Walt McKechnie, who was drafted off the Leafs' roster by Minnesota in the 1967 Expansion Draft, played for six NHL teams before reaching the Leafs in 1978-79.

2. Bill Carson, a 20-goal scorer in 1927-28, was the first Leaf to score wearing the now familiar blue and white.

3. Glenn Anderson spent a season with the Canadian National Team before joining the Edmonton Oilers in 1980-81.

4. Rick Wamsley allowed only eight goals in 253 minutes in his NHL debut with the Montreal Canadiens in 1980-81.

5. Mike Foligno's 36 goals as a rookie was the second-highest total of his career.

6. Laurie Boschman, who had a number of fine seasons with Winnipeg, was traded from Toronto because Harold Ballard felt his Christian beliefs would hinder his aggressiveness. He had 200 penalty minutes three times in his career.

7. Despite becoming the first University of Minnesota Golden Gopher to compile 100 points in a season, Aaron Broten did not receive any post-season awards in 1981. He came to the Leafs in a trade with Quebec in 1991.

8. Brian Curran registered 301 penalty minutes in 1989-90, his only full season with the team.

9. Jamie Macoun's comeback from life-threatening injuries is a remarkable story. He continues to be one of the league's best defencemen.

10. Kent Manderville scored his first NHL goal during the Leafs' 6-0 win over St. Louis in game seven of the Norris Division finals.

11. Rob Ramage, the first player selected in the newly named Entry Draft in 1979, captained the Leafs in 1990 and 1991.

12. Al Secord, a 50-goal scorer with Chicago in 1982-83, registered 221 penalty minutes with the Leafs in 1987-88.

13. Bill Thoms scored 23 goals to tie teammate Charlie Conacher for the NHL lead in goals. He never scored more than 15 goals again.

14. Sid Smith, a two-time winner of the Lady Byng Trophy, led the Leafs in goals scored from 1950-51 to 1954-55.

15. Ron Ward, who scored two goals in 89 NHL games, had four seasons with at least 30 goals in the WHA.

16. Stan Weir scored 33 goals for the Oilers in their first season, the third-highest total on the team.

17. Garth Boesch, an underrated defenceman who played on three Cup winners, retired following the 1950 season.

18. Mike Murphy, a Leafs assistant coach, had five seasons with more than 20 goals for the Los Angeles Kings.

19. John Anderson, who scored 282 goals in the NHL, has also had a very successful minor-league career, compiling 80 points in 65 games for the IHL's San Diego Gulls in 1992-93.

20. John Gibson, who arrived from the Los Angeles Kings for Ian Turnbull, played for five different teams in 1981-82.

21. Bob Manno, the Vancouver Canucks' first selection in the 1976 Amateur Draft, returned to the NHL and played a pair of seasons with Detroit.

22. Terry Martin, originally a Buffalo Sabre, also played with Quebec, Edmonton, and Minnesota.

23. Willie Marshall had fifteen 20-goal seasons in the AHL, playing with Rochester, Baltimore, Providence, Hershey, and Pittsburgh. He played his last NHL game in 1958-59 and became the AHL's all-time leader in games, goals, assists, and points in 1972.

24. Ron Wilson, a Toronto native who was an assistant coach in the Vancouver Canucks' system, became the first coach of the Ducks in June 1993.

25. Bill Sutherland scored 20 goals for the Flyers in their first season and later skated with Detroit and St. Louis.

26. Gordie Bell, one of four Leaf goalies in the 1945-46 season, was recalled by the Rangers in the 1956 playoffs, and led the Rangers to their first victory over Montreal at the Forum since January 30, 1954.

27. Ben Grant, who spent five games with the New York Americans in 1933-34, played in the minors until

1943, when the Leafs promoted him to replace army-bound Turk Broda.

28. Luke Richardson, who was traded to the Edmonton Oilers in the Grant Fuhr deal, knocked Granato so far off his game, the Rangers traded him to Los Angeles.

29. Harold "Baldy" Cotton, who scored 21 goals in 1929-30, played for the Leafs until the 1935-36 season, when he was sold to the New York Americans.

30. Red Horner was first signed to play with the Toronto Marlies, and actually played an afternoon game with that team before making his NHL debut with Toronto that night.

31. Melville "Butch" Keeling reached double figures in goals in seven of his ten years with the Rangers.

32. Ed Joyal, who arrived in Toronto from Detroit in the Andy Bathgate trade, never scored in his 14 games with the Leafs, but he went on to have fine seasons in Los Angeles and in the WHA.

33. Peter Zezel has played pro soccer for the Toronto Blizzard of the NAHL and the North York Rockets of the CSL in addition to his on-ice duties with the Toronto Maple Leafs.

34. Now in his second stint with the Leafs, Mark Osborne's 67 points led all Red Wing scorers in 1981-82. Osborne was sent to the Rangers before he was dealt to Toronto during the 1986-87 campaign.

35. Greg Johnston was traded to the New York Rangers by the Bruins for Chris Nilan on June 28, 1990. Later the same day, he was dealt to the Leafs for Tie Domi.

36. Vincent Damphousse collected 94 points in 1989-90 to erase the Big M's record established in 1960-61.

37. Craig Muni, who was signed as a free agent by

Edmonton and traded from Edmonton to Buffalo and from Buffalo to Pittsburgh and from Pittsburgh back to Edmonton, all in the space of three days. He played on three Cup-winners with the Oilers.

38. Bill Derlago scored 40 goals in the 1983-84 season, only five shy of Sittler's all-time team mark for centres.

39. Walt Poddubny, traded to the Rangers for Mike Allison, had three consecutive seasons with at least 38 goals after leaving the Leafs in 1986-87.

9

Famous Firsts and Lasts

Historically, the toronto maple leafs have long been considered table-setters on the ice, but an equal number of "firsts" have originated in their home, Maple Leaf Gardens. The Carlton Street Cathedral was the most modern of all hockey hotbeds when it was built during the height of the Depression. It was the first NHL rink to have completely clear sight lines, with no pillars obstructing the fans' view, and the first to provide a gondola overlooking the ice surface for radio broadcasts.

The Gardens was also renowned as the first arena to use plexiglass instead of screens around the boards. Although the "shoot-and-scoot" system of throwing the puck into the offensive zone and skating after it had been introduced by the Detroit Red Wings during the 1942 finals, the introduction of plexiglass made this practice more popular, because the bounce off the wire mesh was unpredictable at best. Not surprisingly, the Gardens was also the first arena to have to deal with broken plexiglass, which occurred when the heel of Maurice Richard's skate shattered the glass during the 1948-49 season, captured in a famous picture by the Turofsky Brothers the very moment the glass splintered.

The Leafs were also the first team to use escalators to deliver fans to their seats. On the other side of the ledger, the Leafs were the first team to introduce five different ticket prices, depending on the colour of the seat purchased. Maple Leaf Gardens was also the first arena to separate the penalty boxes, giving each team its own special sin-bin. Prior to the 1962 season, both teams shared the same penalty box, which made for some interesting off-ice shenanigans.

In February 1934, the first NHL All-Star Game was played in Maple Leaf Gardens, as a benefit for the family of Ace Bailey, who had suffered a career-ending head injury. When the league decided to hold an annual All-Star Game in 1947, the first match was held in Maple Leaf Gardens, with a team of NHL All-Stars defeating the Stanley Cup-champion Maple Leafs 4-3.

The Leafs were also the first professional sports team whose games could be heard across Canada on radio, making Foster Hewitt's "He shoots, he scores!" the most famous four words in Canada. When television was introduced in the early 1950s, the first English-language hockey broadcast to be seen coast-to-coast originated from the Carlton Street Cathedral.

Of course, the Gardens was also a celebrated stage for non-hockey events. The opera was a common feature during the summer, transforming the arena from a musty hockey rink into a glorious concert hall for the first time in Canadian music history. In the 1950s, Elvis Presley performed one of the very few concerts of his career outside the United States at Maple Leaf Gardens. In the 1960s, both the Beatles and the Louisville Lip, Muhammad Ali (then known as Cassius Clay), performed at the Carlton Street cashbox to sold out audiences. Still, for all these happenings, the Gardens remains best known as the locale for some of hockey's greatest achievements.

Today, with state-of-the-art training facilities and private and corporate boxes, the Gardens belies the fact it is now 62 years old. In many ways it's not getting older, it's getting better.

Questions

1. Who was the first Maple Leaf to score 40 or more goals in a season?
2. Who was the first Leaf goaltender to register an assist?
3. Who was the first Leaf player to score 50 goals in a season?
4. Who was the first Leaf player to compile 100 points in a season?
5. Who was the first Maple Leaf centreman to be selected to the NHL's All-Star Team?
6. Who was the first Maple Leaf to lead the league in scoring?
7. Who was the first goaltender to record a shutout against the Toronto Maple Leafs?
8. Name the first team the Maple Leafs defeated.

9. Who was the first Leaf to record 50 assists in a season?

10. Who was the first Maple Leaf to score 30 goals in a single season?

11. Who scored the first goal in the history of the Maple Leaf franchise?

12. Who scored the first regular-season winning goal in franchise history?

13. Who was the first Maple Leaf to score four goals in the same period?

14. Who was the first Leaf to lead the team in goals, assists, and points in the same season?

15. Who was the first European to lead the Leafs in scoring?

16. Who was the first Leaf to lead the team in goals and penalty minutes in the same season?

17. Who was the first player to appear in 1,000 games as a Maple Leaf?

18. Who was the first Maple Leaf to score five goals in a game?

19. Who was the first Maple Leaf to score six goals in a single game?

20. Who was the first Leaf rookie to score five goals in one game?

21. Who was the last Maple Leaf to lead the league in scoring?

22. Who was the last Leaf to lead the league in goals scored?

23. Who was the last Leaf to capture the Hart Trophy as league MVP?

24. This former Leaf was the last man to lead the WHA in penalty minutes. Who was the sin-bin king?

25. Who was the last Leaf goaltender to lead the league in goals-against average prior to Felix Potvin in 1992-93?

26. Who was the last Maple Leaf goaltender to lead the league in shutouts?

27. Who was the last Maple Leaf to lead the league in assists?

28. Who was the last Leaf to win a regular-season award in the NHL prior to the 1992-93 season?

29. Who was the coach of the first Leaf team to finish last overall in the NHL standings?

30. Who was the coach of the last Leaf team to finish last in the NHL standings?

31. Who was the last Maple Leaf to score a regular-season hat-trick for the team?

32. Who was the last Leaf to score on a penalty shot?

33. Who was the last coach's son to play for the Maple Leafs?

34. Who was the last player who played for the Leafs to be elected to the Hockey Hall of Fame?

35. Who was the last Leaf goaltender to play without a face mask?

Answers

1. Frank Mahovlich scored 48 goals in 1960-61.

2. Johnny Bower assisted on a Frank Mahovlich goal in a 7-2 win over Boston on February 24, 1962.

3. Rick Vaive scored his 50th goal of the 1981-82 season against St. Louis's Mike Liut on March 24, 1982.

4. Darryl Sittler reached the 100-point plateau on April 3, 1976, in a 4-2 loss to Boston.

5. Syl Apps was the first, and only, Maple Leaf centre to earn a spot on the NHL's All-Star Team.

6. Ace Bailey led the NHL in points in 1928-29 with 22 goals and 10 assists for 32 points.

7. Alex Connell shut out the newly named Maple Leafs 2-0 on March 19, 1927.

8. Toronto beat the New York Americans 4-1 in their first game as the Leafs on February 17, 1927

9. Red Kelly assisted on 50 goals during the 1960-61 season.

10. Charlie Conacher scored 31 goals for the Leafs during the 1930-31 season.

11. Pat Patterson, who played only 29 games with Toronto in his brief career, scored the first Maple Leaf goal on February 17, 1927, on an assist from Bert Corbeau.

12. Ace Bailey scored the Leafs' second goal in their 4-1 victory over the New York Americans in the first game as the Maple Leafs.

13. "Busher" Jackson fired four shots past St. Louis Eagles goaltender Bill Beveridge on November 20, 1934.

14. Ted Kennedy collected 28 goals and 32 assists to lead the team with 60 points in 1946-47.

15. Miroslav Frycer led the Leafs in scoring with 75 points in 1985-86.

16. Tod Sloan scored 37 goals in 1955-56 and registered 100 penalty minutes to lead the team in both statistical categories.

17. Tim Horton reached the 1000-games-played plateau

during the 1968-69 season, just ahead of George Armstrong.

18. Charlie Conacher scored five goals against Roy Worters and the New York Americans on January 19, 1932.

19. Darryl Sittler is the first – and only – Leaf player to score a double hat-trick, sliding half a dozen pucks behind Boston's Dave Reece on February 7, 1976.

20. Howie Meeker set an NHL rookie record by scoring five times in a 10-4 win over Chicago on January 8, 1947.

21. Gordie Drillon won the Art Ross Trophy in 1938 with 26 goals and 26 assists.

22. Gaye Stewart's 37 goals in 1945-46 led the league.

23. Ted Kennedy, who retired after the season, was selected as the league's MVP in 1954-55.

24. Rick Vaive led the WHA with 248 minutes in penalties in the rival league's final campaign.

25. Jacques Plante recorded a GAA of 1.88 in his first full season wearing the blue and white of the Maple Leafs in 1970-71.

26. Harry Lumley, who blanked the opposition 13 times during the 1953-54 season, was the last Leaf shutout King.

27. Syl Apps assisted on 29 goals in the 1937-38 season to become the last Maple Leaf set-up artist.

28. Brit Selby captured the Calder Trophy as the league's rookie of the year in 1965-66, despite compiling only 27 points.

29. Billy Reay's 1957-58 Leaf team finished last in the NHL standings with a 21-38-11 record.

30. With Dan Maloney behind the bench, the Leafs

finished last in the league with a mark of 20-52-8 in 1983-84.

31. Glenn Anderson fired three goals against the Quebec Nordiques in a 4-3 victory on March 17, 1992.

32. Rick Vaive scored against Derren Eliot of the Los Angeles Kings in a 4-3 loss on December 3, 1986.

33. Terry Clancy, who started his NHL career with Oakland, played 91 games for the Leafs between 1969 and 1973. Brent Imlach, who appeared in three NHL games with the Leafs, is the only player in franchise history to actually be coached by his father.

34. Lanny McDonald earned his place in the Hockey Hall of Fame in 1992.

35. Bruce Gamble didn't start wearing a mask until the 1970-71 season.

Champions

The following six players were all members of Toronto's Stanley Cup winning team in 1967. Can you name them? Answers on page 128.

1

2

3

4

5

6

Famous Quotes

Who delivered these Leaf lines? Answers on page 129.

1. "Hockey is mostly a streetcar named Desire but sometimes Frank misses it."
2. "I wouldn't trade Ian Turnbull for God."
3. "How about for God and a first-round draft choice?"
4. "I'm retiring to go back to the farm and make some real money."
5. "If you can't beat 'em in the alley, you can't beat 'em on the ice."
6. "This is it ... this is the ultimate. I don't think I'll be able to play another game."
7. "Punch couldn't keep his team on an even pitch. It was always struggle, struggle, struggle. Seems to me, those Canadiens teams didn't have to go through that."
8. "My only regret was that I didn't hit the general manager of the Leafs when I had the chance."
9. "We've got to get that cancer out of the dressing room."
10. "I think they convinced themselves that they should win it, that it really should be theirs. But it didn't turn out that way. Our goaltenders got hot. Those things happen."

10

The Rivalry

ALTHOUGH THEY HAVEN'T FACED EACH OTHER IN THE playoffs since 1979, and have met only 13 times in total, the Toronto Maple Leafs–Montreal Canadiens rivalry is one of the greatest in all of professional sport. In the six-team era, the two-team struggle was a natural, since the Habs and Leafs were the only Canadian clubs in the league. But there was more to it than that. The games were a sort of symbolic civil war, culture against culture, system against system, English against French. The fact that in the mid-1940s the Canadiens coach (Dick Irvin) and the team's general manager (Frank Selke) were former Maple Leaf employees only increased the on-ice tension of those early playoff meetings.

The two combatants didn't meet in the post-season until 1944, when Maurice Richard wrote his name in the record book with a five-goal performance in only the second playoff game of his career. The Leafs exacted their revenge the following season, rebounding from a 10-3 thrashing in game five to win the series in six games with a 3-2 victory in the decisive contest. In 1947, the Leafs once again gained the upper hand on the Habs, winning the Stanley Cup with a six-game triumph. Fittingly, the Cup-clinching goal was scored by Ted Kennedy, a product of the Montreal Canadiens' system.

Once again in 1951, the Leafs reigned supreme, winning four overtime games to capture their fourth Stanley Cup in five years. The Leafs and Canadiens met again in the finals in 1959 and 1960, but the rebuilding Leafs had little chance against the powerhouse Canadiens, who were on their way to five consecutive Cup titles.

The most famous Leaf–Canadien skirmishes occurred in the 1960s, when each game was a battle and each series a war. The Leafs won the decade-long altercation 3-2, although only one series was for the championship. That would be the great 1967 confrontation, when the Leafs ruined the Canadiens' plans to celebrate their marvellous Expo '67 World's Fair by winning the Cup in six games.

Since that time, the Canadiens have dominated the Leafs, winning both playoff series and the majority of the regular-season matches. In fact, the Leafs haven't defeated the Canadiens in the post-season since that evening in May 1967 when George Armstrong's empty-net goal cemented the Leafs' last Cup victory. Yet, regardless of the quality of the team, the prospect of playing the Canadiens often brings out the best in the Leaf players. Although the teams now meet only twice a year, those games are circled on the calendar months in advance and there's an electricity in the air before the opening faceoff that is absent in most regular-season matches.

The 1992-93 season was extra special for all hockey fans. The Leafs were rebuilding with former Canadiens coach Pat Burns at the helm and the Toronto–Montreal confrontations were two of the most exciting matches of the schedule. Unfortunately, the treasured post-season meeting never came to be as the Leafs came within one goal of meeting the Canadiens on the most storied of battle fronts – the Stanley Cup finals. Still, with three former Leafs in the Montreal lineup and francophone stars like Felix Potvin and Sylvain Lefebvre on the Toronto roster, the long awaited post-season rematch of the cultures and languages could become a reality someday soon.

Questions

1. Name the three players who won five consecutive Stanley Cup championships with the Montreal Canadiens in the 1950s and later played for the Leafs.
2. What was the date and score of the last time the Leafs defeated the Montreal Canadiens in a playoff game?
3. In the last Leafs–Habs playoff game, the Canadiens won in overtime on a powerplay goal. Who scored the winner and which Leaf watched it from the penalty box?
4. When did the Maple Leafs and Canadiens first meet in the post-season and what was the series score?

5. In the 1945 playoffs, Toronto won the pivotal fourth game to take a commanding 3-1 lead in games. Who scored the overtime winner for the Leafs?

6. In game four of the 1965 semi-finals, Punch Imlach devised his own method of discussing the on-ice activity with referee Art Skov. What did he do?

7. How many times have the Leafs and Canadiens met in the playoffs and what is the series score?

8. This former Art Ross Trophy-winning Maple Leaf finished his career with the Canadiens. Who is he?

9. Who are the three players to lead both the Maple Leafs and the Montreal Canadiens in scoring?

10. The only player to wear the number "0" for the Montreal Canadiens also played for the Toronto Maple Leafs. Who was this neutral-numbered net-minder?

11. In 1944, the Montreal Canadiens went undefeated at home during the regular season. However, in the first game of the playoffs, the Leafs shocked the Canadiens with a victory on Forum ice. Who scored the winning goal for the Leafs and what was the score?

12. Of the 33 players who appeared in a Leafs uniform in 1992-93, two had played for the Montreal Canadiens. Can you name them?

13. The Stanley Cup-champion Montreal Canadiens had three former Leafs in their lineup during the 1992-93 season. Name them.

14. This former Montreal Canadiens star was the first player to be named an assistant coach by the Leafs. Can you name him?

15. Another former Canadiens star, a two-time winner of the Art Ross Trophy, played for the Leafs during the 1964-65 season. Name him.

16. Who were the principals in the first trade between the Leafs and the Canadiens and when did the deal take place?

17. Who was the first player to suit up for both the Montreal Canadiens and the Toronto Maple Leafs in the same season?

18. Five players who have played for both the Leafs and Habs are in the Hockey Hall of Fame. Name them.

19. Frank Mahovlich wore number 27 for both the Leafs and the Canadiens. However, when he arrived in Montreal during the 1970-71 season, he wore another number. What was that number and why did the Big M wear it?

20. Who was the all-time Montreal Canadien great who was signed by the Leafs in 1937, but never played for them?

21. Early in the 1942-43 season, "Rocket" Richard replaced a former Leaf forward on a line with Elmer Lach and Toe Blake, signalling the start of Montreal's famed "Punch Line." Who was the player Richard replaced?

22. In the 1947 finals between Montreal and Toronto, a key member of the Habs was suspended for a game for intent to injure. Who was the suspended player and whom did he attack?

23. Who was the executive who helped build both the Leafs and the Canadiens into NHL powerhouses?

24. One of the greatest players ever to skate with the

Canadiens started his career with the Quebec Aces. The Aces, in turn, were then coached by a future Leaf GM. Who were the two future NHL leaders?

25. Only two men have coached both the Montreal Canadiens and the Toronto Maple Leafs. Who are they?

26. This goaltender, who played for both the Leafs and the Canadiens, is the only netminder to be traded midway through a season in which he won the Vezina Trophy. Who is he?

27. This former Toronto forward, who actually started his career as a defenceman, was a member of the Montreal Canadiens Stanley Cup-winning team in 1993. Name him.

28. During the 1951 finals between Toronto and Montreal, all five games went into overtime. Four Leafs scored the only overtime goals of their career in that series. Can you name the Leaf scorers and the lone marksman for the Canadiens?

29. The key to the Leafs' future was solidified in 1942, when they obtained one of their greatest players from the Montreal Canadiens. Name the player the Leafs sent to the Habs and the player they received in exchange.

30. In game one of the 1947 finals, the Montreal Canadiens trounced the Leafs 6-0, leading one Canadien to ask, "How did those guys ever make the playoffs?" The quote woke up the Leafs and they won the series in six games to capture their fourth Stanley Cup. Which Hab made the ill-timed remark?

31. On Christmas Eve, 1931, the Leafs and Canadiens thought they had played to a 1-1 overtime draw

when it was discovered the timekeeper had ended the game 10 seconds early. The teams returned to the ice, and the Leafs scored in the remaining time. Who scored the goal and who won the centre-ice draw to set up the winning marker?

32. A former Leaf defenceman, I played on the 1949 championship club with Toronto before being traded to Montreal, where I played in the 1951 finals. I never played in the NHL again. Who am I?

33. The Leafs acquired Stan Smyrke from Montreal for this player, who later coached the Habs to a Stanley Cup championship. Who was the future Cup-winning coach?

34. On December 17, 1982, the Leafs acquired two players from the Canadiens in two separate transactions. Can you name the two players the Leafs received?

35. Since 1967, two Maple Leaf goaltenders have recorded their first career shutouts against the Montreal Canadiens. Can you name them and the year they blanked the Habs?

Answers

1. Don Marshall, Dickie Moore, and Jacques Plante all played for the Leafs late in their careers.

2. Toronto defeated the Montreal Canadiens 3-1 on May 2, 1967, to win the Stanley Cup.

3. Larry Robinson scored at 4:14 of overtime with Tiger Williams in the penalty box. After Robinson scored, Williams stormed out of the box and attempted to

attack referee Bob Myers, but Robinson intervened and held Williams back.

4. The Montreal Canadiens defeated Toronto four games to one in their first meeting in the 1944 semi-finals.

5. Gus Bodnar scored at 12:36 of overtime to put the Leafs a single victory away from the Stanley Cup finals.

6. During a lengthy delay in game four of the semi-finals, Imlach donned a pair of skates and stood in the doorway of the players bench, threatening to join the fray on the ice.

7. The Leafs and Habs have met 13 times in the post-season, with the Canadiens holding a slim 7-6 lead, including six of the last eight series.

8. Gordie Drillon had a career-high 28 goals for Montreal in 1942-43, his only season with the Habs and his last campaign in the NHL. He joined the army the next season and decided to return to New Brunswick after the War, where he played senior hockey for the Saint John Beavers and the Moncton Hawks.

9. Frank Mahovlich, Russ Courtnall, and Vincent Damphousse have led both the Leafs and Canadiens in scoring during their careers.

10. Paul Bibeault, who many critics said played like his number (zero), appeared in 110 games for the Habs and 29 games for the Leafs.

11. George Boothman, who scored just two playoff goals in his career, fired the winning tally in the Leafs' 3-1 victory in the opening game of the 1944 semi-finals. It was Toronto's only victory in the series.

12. Sylvain Lefebvre and Rick Wamsley both started their careers with the Montreal Canadiens.

13. Rob Ramage, Vincent Damphousse, and Gary Leeman are all Maple Leaf alumni.

14. Bert Olmstead was named as an assistant coach when Punch Imlach took over the Leafs' coaching reins in December 1958.

15. Dickie Moore, who set an NHL record with 96 points in 1959, played 38 games with the Leafs in 1964-65.

16. In 1933, the Leafs sent goaltender Lorne Chabot to the Montreal Canadiens for goaltender Georges Hainsworth. The deal took 10 seconds to complete. In a telephone conversation, the Habs asked for Chabot and offered Hainsworth. Smythe said, "OK, we'll announce it tomorrow," and hung up.

17. Robert Picard started the 1980-81 season for the Leafs before being traded to the Montreal Canadiens for Michel Larocque.

18. Georges Hainsworth, Jacques Plante, Bert Olmstead, Frank Mahovlich, and Dickie Moore are all in the Hall of Fame.

19. Mahovlich was traded to Montreal on January 13, 1971, and joined the team in Minnesota. He wore number 10 that evening because there was no jersey number 27 available. No one wore number 10 again that year, so the Big M was the last Montreal Canadien to wear number 10 before the great Guy Lafleur.

20. Elmer Lach was signed by Toronto in 1937 but later traded to the New York Rangers because he was too small, a "peanut" according to Conn Smythe. Lach

refused to report to the Rangers, was granted free agency, and signed with Montreal.

21. Charlie Sands, who spent two seasons with the Leafs, played only a handful of games for the Canadiens after Richard replaced him on the line with Blake and Lach. Sands was also the last position player to play goal for the Canadiens, taking over in net for an injured Wilf Cude on February 22, 1939.

22. Maurice Richard was suspended for game three after cutting Vic Lynn and Bill Ezinicki with his stick. Without the Rocket in the lineup, the Habs dropped a 4-2 decision to the Leafs, who went on to win the Cup in five games.

23. Frank Selke, Sr., who joined the Leafs in 1929 and helped them to three Cup wins, joined the Montreal Canadiens in 1947 and led that franchise to seven Stanley Cup wins.

24. Jean Beliveau spent two seasons with the Quebec Aces of the Quebec Senior Hockey League before joining the Canadiens. His coach was the future leader of the Leafs, Punch Imlach.

25. Dick Irvin coached the Leafs from 1931-32 to 1939-40 and led the Montreal Canadiens from 1940-41 to 1954-55. Pat Burns coached the Habs from 1988-89 to 1991-92 and was appointed as the Leafs coach on May 29, 1992.

26. Michel "Bunny" Larocque was traded from the Montreal Canadiens to the Leafs in March, 1981.

27. Gary Leeman, who captured the WHL's Defenceman of the Year award in 1982, was switched to forward by Mike Nykoluk and became just the second Leaf to

score 50 goals in a season. He was traded to Montreal in 1993 and won the Stanley Cup with the bleu, blanc, et rouge.

28. The four sudden-death marksmen for Toronto were Sid Smith (game one, 5:51 of overtime), Ted Kennedy (game three, 4:47 of overtime), Harry Watson (game four, 5:15 of overtime), and Bill Barilko (game five, 2:53 of overtime). Maurice Richard countered for Montreal at 2:55 of overtime in game two.

29. The Leafs received Ted Kennedy from Montreal in exchange for Frank Eddolls. The move was completed by Frank Selke without Conn Smythe's permission, creating tension between the two men that ultimately led to Selke's resignation.

30. Bill Durnan, the last goaltender to serve as captain of an NHL team, made the offhand remark that motivated the Leafs.

31. "Busher" Jackson took a left-wing feed from Joe Primeau to win the game for the Leafs. Howie Morenz, who lost the faceoff to Primeau, avenged the loss two nights later by scoring one overtime goal and setting up Aurel Joliat for another in a 2-0 overtime win for the Habs.

32. Bobby Dawes, who suffered a broken leg in a game against Toronto earlier in the year, was moved to forward in game five of the 1951 finals, his final NHL game.

33. Al MacNeil, who spent only one season with Montreal, returned to the organization and coached the Canadiens to their upset Cup victory in 1970-71.

34. The Leafs received Dan Daoust and Gaston Gingras

from the Montreal Canadiens for future draft choices.

35. Mike Palmateer blanked Montreal 1-0 on November 17, 1976, to record his first NHL shutout while Felix Potvin whitewashed the Habs 4-0 on January 23, 1993, for his first career zero.

Word Puzzle

Find words in letter puzzle below. Words can be found horizontally, vertically, diagonally, spelled frontward or backward. Solution on page 130.

```
O D U N C W I L S O N B R A Y
T O D D G I L L E N T R I C N
N E Z B L U E L I N E A C L E
O M X B E N T C Y B O D U I G
R E K E E M E I W O H M V F N
O J C A I R I C O A H A C F I
T O R I C K V A I V E R A F M
A H O M I E N E I K R S I L L
D N E T W F B R A L K H S E A
U C H A S H C A O C H R S T S
N U A R H C I R I J O N D C E
A L I A F R A T E L I N R H J
P L A L I A S T I K E B A E R
Q E M A X B E N T L E Y O R O
B N R Y X D R O F L U P B O B
```

Ace Bailey	Cliff Fletcher	John Cullen
Al Iafrate	Coach	Max Bentley
Blueline	Dunc Wilson	Net
Boards	Howie Meeker	Rick Vaive
Bob Pulford	Ice	Stick
Borje Salming	Jiri Chra	Todd Gill
Brad Marsh		Toronto

123

Answers

Page 35

1 (c), 2 (g), 3 (d), 4 (a), 5 (i), 6 (h), 7 (e), 8 (b), 9 (f).

Page 49

1 (v), 2 (c), 3 (u), 4 (e), 5 (l), 6 (s), 7 (w), 8 (n), 9 (r),
10 (x), 11 (m), 12 (b), 13 (j), 14 (y), 15 (q), 16 (e), 17
(d), 18 (g), 19 (t), 20 (h), 21 (p), 22 (a), 23 (k), 24
(o), 25 (i).

Page 60

Day	1940-41 to 1949-50
Kelly	1973-74 to 1976-77
Meeker	1956-57
Maloney	1984-85 to 1985-86
Primeau	1950-51 to 1952-53
Neilson	1977-78 to 1978-79

Page 73

1. Alexander Godynyuk   Calgary
2. Claude Loiselle   NY Islanders

3. Dave Hannan	Buffalo
4. Daniel Marois	NY Islanders
5. Jeff Reese	Calgary
6. Tom Fergus	Vancouver

Page 87

1961-62
   Eddie Shack, Bob Pulford

1962-63
   Kent Douglas, Ron Stewart

1963-64
   Jim Pappin, Gerry Ehman

1966-67
   Marcel Pronovost, Milan Marcetta

Pages 88-9

ACROSS

1. STEMKOWSKI (Pete Stemkowski)
5. PG (Paul Gardner)
7. BG (Bruce Gamble)
9. GILMOUR (Doug Gilmour)
12. ALARM
13. NATURE
15. ET (Errol Thompson)
16. PAID
19. LC (Lorne Chabot)
20. IMLACH (Punch Imlach)
22. FELIX (Felix Potvin)
24. MS (Marian Statsny)
25. ELLIS (Ron Ellis)

26. CONN (Conn Smythe)
28. LANNY (Lanny McDonald)
29. CLANCY (King Clancy)
30. DW (Dave Williams)
31. FIVE
32. JR (Jeff Reese)
33. ANKLE
35. PUCK
38. TIM (Tim Horton)
39. LEY (Rick Ley)
41. DAN (Dan Daoust)
42. BAR
43. COURTNALL (Russ Courtnall)
46. RUSH
47. OT (Overtime)
48. DD (Dick Duff)
49. KEON (Dave Keon)
51. APPS (Syl Apps)
55. ING (Peter Ing)
57. TURNBULL (Ian Turnbull)
58. TURK (Turk Broda)
59. TK (Ted Kennedy)
60. EAST (East Division)
63. ICE
66. MALONEY (Dan Maloney)
67. HD (Hap Day)
68. ANDREYCHUK (Dave Andreychuk)

DOWN

1. STANLEY CUP
2. MORRISON (Jim Morrison)
3. WIN
4. KITCHEN (Mike Kitchen)
5. PI (Peter Ihnacak)
6. GL (Gary Leeman)
7. BO (Bert Olmstead)
8. GU (Garry Unger)
10. MAPLE LEAF GARDENS
11. RED (Leonard "Red" Kelly)
14. RON LOW
17. AI (Al Iafrate)
18. IX (Nine)
21. LUCY
23. GUY (Guy Trottier)
27. NORM (Norm Ullman)
31. FAVELL (Doug Favell)
32. JIM (Jim McKenny)
34. ES (Eddie Shack)
36. CLARK (Wendel Clark)

Page 109

1. Larry Hillman
2. Allan Stanley
3. Mike Walton
4. Brian Conacher
5. Larry Jeffrey
6. Jim Pappin

Page 110

1. Punch Imlach on Frank Mahovlich's lack of motivation, 1965

2. Harold Ballard, replying to trade talk about defenceman Ian Turnbull, 1978.

3. Roger Neilson's reply to Ballard's holy orders regarding Turnbull.

4. Garth Boesch, upon his retirement after the 1949-50 season.

5. Conn Smythe's battle cry, 1938.

6. Terry Sawchuk after the Leafs won the Cup, May 2, 1967.

7. Frank Mahovlich, 1989.

8. Lanny McDonald after being traded to Colorado, December 28, 1979.

9. Harold Ballard on Darryl Sittler, 1980.

10. Dave Keon, discussing the 1967 Stanley Cup finals, 1990.

O D U N C W I L S O N B R A Y
T O D D G I L L E N T R I C N
N E Z B L U E L I N E A C L E
O M X B E N T C Y B O D U I G
R E K E E M E I W O H M V F N
O J C A I R I C O A H A C F I
T O R I C K V A I V E R A F M
A H O M I E N E I K R S I L L
D N E T W F B R A L K H S E A
U C H A S H C A O C H R S T S
N U A R H C I R I J O N D C E
A L I A F R A T E L I N R H J
P L A L I A S T I K E B A E R
Q E M A X B E N T L E Y O R O
B N R Y X D R O F L U P B O B